John Gilmary Shea

The Life of Pope Pius IX. and the great Events in the History of the Church during his Pontificate

John Gilmary Shea

The Life of Pope Pius IX. and the great Events in the History of the Church during his Pontificate

ISBN/EAN: 9783743305687

Manufactured in Europe, USA, Canada, Australia, Japa

Cover: Foto ©ninafisch / pixelio.de

Manufactured and distributed by brebook publishing software (www.brebook.com)

John Gilmary Shea

The Life of Pope Pius IX. and the great Events in the History of the Church during his Pontificate

THE LIFE

OF

POPE PIUS IX.

AND THE

GREAT EVENTS IN THE HISTORY OF THE CHURCH
DURING HIS PONTIFICATE.

By JOHN GILMARY SHEA, LL.D.

NEW YORK:
THOMAS KELLY.
1877.

Copyright by
THOMAS KELLY,
1877.

Printed by Thomas Kelly,
New York.

Imprimatur,

✠ JOHN, CARDINAL McCLOSKEY,
Archbishop of New York.

Approbation and Commendations of the Life of Pope Pius IX., by John Gilmary Shea, LL.D., Published by Thomas Kelly, 17 Barclay Street, New York.

APPROBATION OF HIS EMINENCE CARDINAL McCLOSKEY.

IMPRIMATUR

✠ JOHN CARDINAL McCLOSKEY,
Archbishop of New York.

ARCHBISHOP PURCELL OF CINCINNATI.

MR. THOMAS KELLY:

Thanks for your copy of the LIFE OF PIUS IX., by the distinguished author J. G. Shea. . . . We cannot, I am sure, fail to be instructed and delighted with Mr. Shea's volume. Please offer my felicitations to the gifted, zealous author.

J. B. PURCELL,
Archbishop of Cincinnati.

BISHOP GILMOUR OF CLEVELAND.

I hope that the publication of so excellent a work may be remunerative to you and of advantage to the reading public, who pretend to know so much, yet know so little, concerning the great and gloriously reigning Pius IX.

✠ R. GILMOUR,
Bishop of Cleveland.

BISHOP TÖBBE OF COVINGTON.

Covington, Ky., August 5th, 1877.

THOMAS KELLY, Esq.,
New York.

DEAR SIR:

I am happy to learn that our Catholic literature will be enriched by a Life of our glorious Holy Father, from the eminent pen of John Gilmary Shea, a writer so well known to the Catholic public, that his very name carries with it a guarantee for the excellence of any work from his pen.

What a rare treat may we not expect from him, when applying himself to so glorious a subject!

May the volume on the life of Pio Nono find a hearty welcome in every Catholic family of the land; such is the fervent desire of,

Yours truly in Christ,

✠ A. M. TÖBBE,
Bishop of Covington.

Approbation and Commendations of the Life of Pope Pius IX., by John Gilmary Shea, LL.D., Published by Thomas Kelly, 17 Barclay Street, New York.

ARCHBISHOP WOOD OF PHILADELPHIA.

MR. THOMAS KELLY:

The Archbishop desires to thank Mr. Kelly for this beautiful work, entirely worthy of the illustrious subject and the author.

✠ J. F. WOOD,
Archbishop of Philadelphia.

BISHOP DWENGER OF FORT WAYNE.

Many thanks for the beautiful copy of the LIFE OF POPE PIUS IX., from the gifted pen of J. G. Shea.

✠ JOSEPH DWENGER,
Bishop of Fort Wayne.

BISHOP GIBBONS OF RICHMOND.

The interest felt by the Catholic world in the illustrious subject of the biography, and the well-known literary reputation of the author, cannot fail to secure for the work a wide circulation, which, I trust, will reward your laudable enterprise.

JAMES GIBBONS,
Bishop of Richmond.

BISHOP MULLEN OF ERIE.

The LIFE OF PIUS IX., by J. G. Shea, is, like all the productions of the gifted author, a work of great merit, while the style in which it is published is in all respects worthy the eminent services rendered to religion by the great Pontiff of whom it treats.

✠ T. MULLEN,
Bishop of Erie.

BISHOP HENDRICKEN OF PROVIDENCE.

The work is issued in a manner most creditable to your house, but not too elegantly for the wonderful and well-told narrative it contains. Mr. John Gilmary Shea has succeeded in compiling a book for which all the Catholics of this country were waiting, and for which he will receive their best thanks.

✠ THOMAS F. HENDRICKEN,
Bishop of Providence.

BISHOP FOLEY OF CHICAGO.

The author is too well known to need any commendation from me, and a true life of Pius IX. necessarily makes a grand and attractive work.

✠ THOMAS FOLEY,
Bishop of Chicago.

PREFACE.

THERE is not a Catholic family in which the little ones do not recognize the portrait of our Holy Father, Pope Pius IX., and look upon it with affection and reverence. The war which the world has waged upon him so unrelentingly as Pope and Prince has drawn all faithful hearts to him, while his piety, charity, patience, and gentleness endear him personally to every Catholic.

There are, unfortunately, few lives of this great Pope in the hands of the people. In time, elaborate works will come rich in documents and illustrations, for those whose leisure permits them to study thoroughly the history of our century: our aim is a modest one: it is simply to give the general reader as vivid a picture as we can in brief of what our loved and venerated Pope has done and suffered and accomplished; to picture his character so as to make it as well known among us as his countenance, and thus rivet more firmly the loyalty and attachment which bind the faithful to the See of Peter and to the two hundred and fifty-eighth of the Sovereign Pontiffs, who began with the Prince of the Apostles.

Catholic princes and governments have ceased to exist: the Church addresses herself to the Catholic hearts of her people: Pope Pius IX. looks to them for the moral support which, under heaven, is to sustain him in his trials, and to these devoted adherents of our beloved Pope we offer our brief sketch.

CONTENTS.

CHAPTER I.
His Birth and Education.—Illness.—Enters the Ecclesiastical State.—Tata Giovanni. —Mission to Chili.—Archbishop of Spoleto.—Bishop of Imola.—Cardinal...... 11

CHAPTER II.
The Election.—Cardinal Mastai Ferretti chosen Pope.—The Ordinance of Amnesty.— The Memorandum of 1831.—Popularity of Pius IX. at Home and Abroad.— Opinions of American Statesmen as to the Pope 57

CHAPTER III.
Pius IX. and the Church at Large.—His First Encyclical.—Promotion of Cardinals.—The Pope in the Pulpit.—Ecclesiastical Reforms.—Ireland. — America.— Religious Orders...................... 79

CHAPTER IV.
The Civil Affairs of Rome.—Italy in a Ferment.—The Fundamental Statute.—The Italian War against Austria.—Defeat of Charles Albert.—Change of Ministry.— Violence of the Revolutionists against the Pope.—The Church in Russia.—Spain.— France............................ 103

CHAPTER V.

The Ministry of Count Rossi.—A United Italy. — Assassination of Rossi. — The Quirinal besieged.—Pius IX. deserted by all but the Diplomatic Corps.—His Escape to Gaeta.—His Reception by the King of Naples...................... 123

CHAPTER VI.

Pius IX. at Gaeta.—His Protest.—Rome in the Hands of the Revolution. — Intervention of the Catholic Powers.—General Oudinot Recovers Rome. — Napoleon's Tortuous Policy.—Pius IX. Invited to America.—Encyclical on the Immaculate Conception.—His Work at Gaeta...... 147

CHAPTER VII.

Pius IX. Restored to Rome.—His Edict of September 12, 1849. — His Return to Rome. —The English Hierarchy. —The Church and the World............... 185

CHAPTER VIII.

The Definition of the Dogma of the Immaculate Conception of the Blessed Virgin Mary.—The Accident at the Church of St. Agnes.—"Immaculate Virgin, Help Us!"............................. 213

CHAPTER IX.

The French War against Austria.—Its Results.—The Sardinians seize Bologna and incite the Legations to Revolt.—Dupli-

CONTENTS.

city of Napoleon III.—The Kingdom of Naples seized. — Victor Emmanuel annexes the Marches and Umbria.—A Papal Army under Lamoriciere attempts to uphold the Pope's Authority.—Castelfidardo.—Ancona Capitulates.—The Maronites of the Lebanon.—Conversions in Bulgaria.—Hostility of the French Government.—The Canonization of the Japanese Martyrs....................... 244

.CHAPTER X.

The Polish Persecution.—Efforts of Pope Pius IX.—The Convention of September 15, 1864.—The Encyclical Quanta Cura and the Syllabus.—Prussia's Progress in Germany. — France Evacuates Rome.—The Centenary of St. Peter.—Canonization of the Martyrs of Gorcum.—Garibaldi renews his Attempts on Rome.—Bad Faith of the Sardinians. — The French return.—Mentana and the Defeat of Garibaldi.......................... 273

CHAPTER XI.

The Golden Jubilee of Pius IX.—The Bull Æterni Patris Convoking the General Council.—The Council of the Vatican.. 302

CHAPTER XII.

Victor Emmanuel invades the Papal Territory.—He takes Rome with an Army of Sixty Thousand Men.—Pius IX. a Prisoner. —His Encyclical denouncing the Act................................ 333

CHAPTER XIII.

The Prisoner of the Vatican.—The Law of Guarantees.—The Encyclical of May, 1871, condemning it.—Peter's Pence.—Its Employment.—The Years of Peter.—The Twenty-fifth Anniversary of his Election and Coronation.............. 354

CHAPTER XIV.

Victor Emmanuel in Rome.—Seizure of the Quirinal.—Devotion of the Romans to Pius IX.—Persecution of the Church in Germany and Switzerland.—The Sacred College.—An Irish Cardinal.—Persecution in Brazil, Russia, and Italy.—An American Cardinal.—The Golden Jubilees................................ 379

CHAPTER XV.

Personal Appearance of Pius IX.—His Mode of Life.—Supernatural Gifts ascribed to Him.—Conclusion.................... 424
Father Burke on Pius IX................. 441

THE LIFE AND TIMES
OF THE
SOVEREIGN PONTIFF PIUS IX.

CHAPTER I.

HIS BIRTH AND EDUCATION.—ILLNESS.—ENTERS THE ECCLESIASTICAL STATE.—TATA GIOVANNI.—MISSION TO CHILI.—ARCHBISHOP OF SPOLETO.—BISHOP OF IMOLA.—CARDINAL.

THERE have been great and illustrious pontificates in the history of the Church, pontificates that stand prominently forth by the personal holiness of the Pope and the great works he accomplished for the Church of God, or the great sufferings he underwent in her defense.

These pontificates mark distinct epochs in ecclesiastical history; and with them posterity will range the remarkable reign of Pius IX. The length of years during which Divine Providence has sustained him in his eminent position; the personal sanctity which breathes forth in all his actions; the zeal with which he has met the spirit of an unbelieving age, that seeks to destroy alike the organization and the faith of the Church; the defining of an article of faith called for by the piety of a world, the convoking of a general council, the heroism and serenity displayed amid the vicissitudes and misfortunes that have chequered his career; exile, spoliation, imprisonment; a great heart afflicted by the sight of the evils visited on those who adhered to him and to the cause of God; all these conspire to invest Pius IX. and his pontificate with a halo peculiarly his own.

Living in the same period, we lose sight, in the daily occurrence of events, of that full view with which history will regard the great Pope of the noontide of the nineteenth century. Hence it becomes necessary to picture it at once to the eyes of the faithful, that grasping the details in a single canvas they may regard with awe the illustrious highpriest who now rules the Church of God on earth.

John Mary Mastai Ferretti was born and baptized at Sinigaglia, in the ancient duchy of Urbino, on the 13th of May, 1792, when France was in the throes of that Revolution which was to convulse Europe and exercise so baleful an influence over the incoming century.

The Mastai family, originally from Crema, in Lombardy, had for six centuries held a prominent position at Sinigaglia, and his father, Count Jerome, gonfalonier of the city, was the heir also of the distinguished family of the Ferretti. His mother, the Countess Catharine Solazzi, illustrated her high rank by her virtues and sound judgment.

The earliest impressions of the child were of the new war of the World on the

Church, his uncle Andrew, the unflinching bishop of Pesaro, having been imprisoned for his fidelity to the Holy See; and the earliest special prayers taught him by his pious mother, being offered up for the deliverance of Pope Pius VI. when that venerable pontiff was a prisoner in the hands of the French. The sympathy of his young heart gave fervor to these prayers, but the pious mother had to remind him of our Saviour's prayer on the cross for his executioners, to unfold to the mind of her son the Christian motives that required him to pray for the persecutors.

Thus in days when the future of religion looked so gloomy, a pious mother prepared by the faithful discharge of her duties a great Pontiff for the Church.

"But, mother," said the boy, "these French who have carried off the Pope are wicked people, are they not? And you make me pray for them?"

"My son, if they are wicked we have

PIUS VI. (JOHN ANGELO BRASCHI.)
Born 1717.
Reigned 1775–1799.

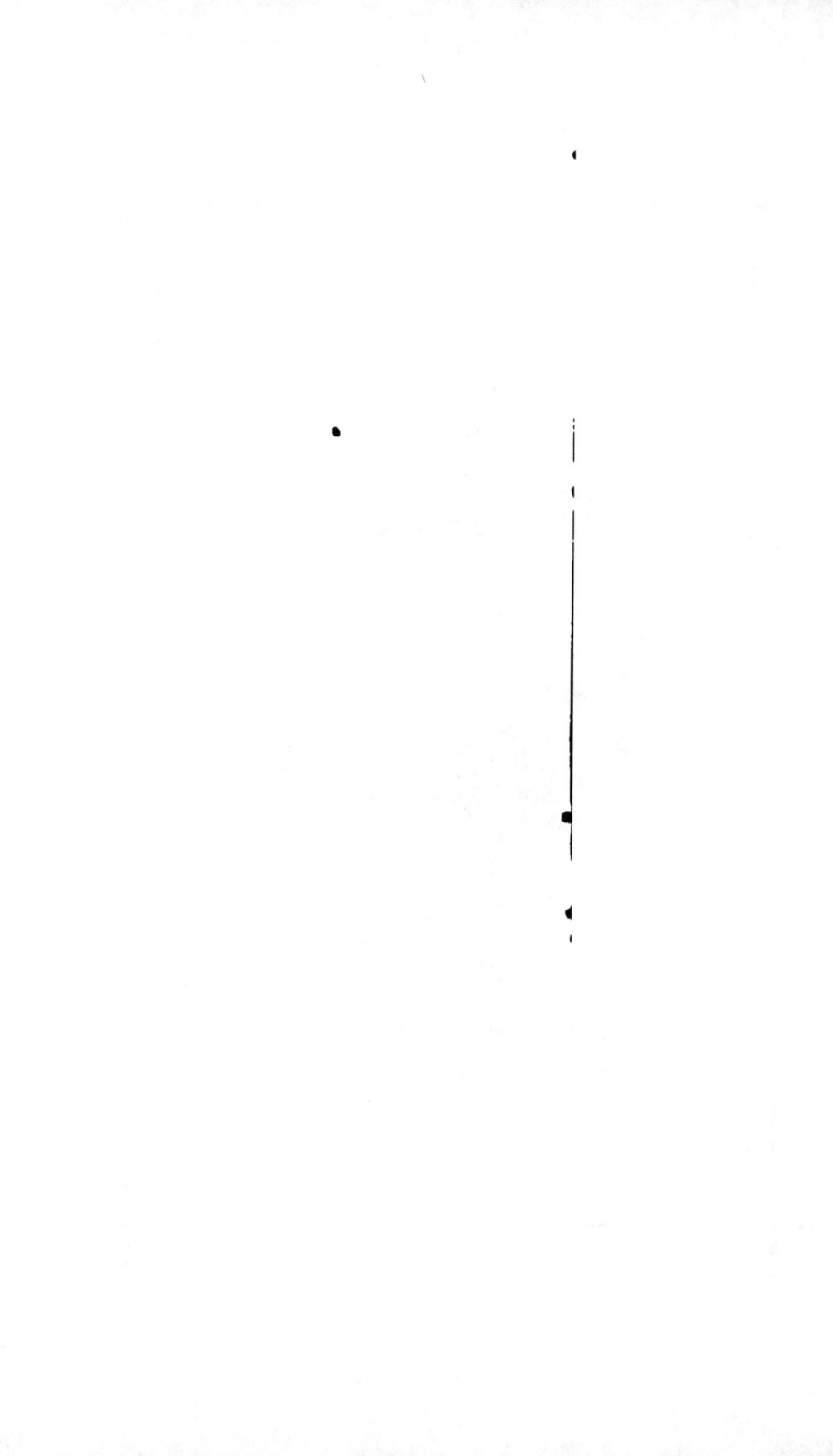

all the more reason to pray for them: but they are not all wicked. It is their government which holds the Pope a prisoner. Their government is wicked."

"And must we pray for that government?"

"Yes, surely. Our Lord prayed for those who crucified him."

In October, 1797, while the family were at a country seat, the young boy was rambling out under the care of a servant. Unperceived by his attendant he ran to the bank of a deep pond, and while eagerly watching the shoals of tiny fish near the bank, lost his balance and fell in. The servant, warned by the splashing of the water, rushed up and rescued the boy; but a fever resulted, followed by a general prostration of strength and ultimately, as we shall see, by serious disease.

When he attained the age of eleven his parents placed him at Volterra, in a college directed by the Fathers of the Pious

Schools, an order founded by Saint Joseph Calasanctius, and which, after the suppression of the Jesuits, endeavored in many parts to replace the colleges of that illustrious body. Young Mastai won esteem with all by his talents and application, by his brilliancy in thought and expression, by that sweetness of disposition, which blended with a firm and noble character never degenerated into weakness. He was prominent among the students, and always selected as a representative pupil by his accomplished teachers when royal personages visited the institution.

He had reached the age of sixteen, and the close of his college course was approaching with its honors, when all hopes of academic success, and of eminence in after life were dashed by a sudden blow. The young student was seized with sudden fits of epilepsy. This seemed to preclude him from embracing the ecclesiastical state to which his wishes and those of his parents had already directed him. The prayer of faith rather than medical skill checked the disease, and in 1809, John Mary Mastai Ferretti received the tonsure at the hands of Monsignor Tecontie, the bishop of Volterra. He then proceeded to Rome, and living in the household of an uncle, Paulinus Mastai, who was a canon in the Vatican Basilica, he entered upon those studies which were to fit him, intellectually, for the priesthood, to which God called him. But he was not long permitted to enjoy the advantages of a training in the great divinity schools of the Capital of the Christian World. In May, of that same year, Napoleon issued a decree dispossessing the Pope of his States, and in July the Holy Father, Pius VII., was torn from the Quirinal by French troops and hurried away a prisoner to Savona.

The young levite withdrew from the

Holy City, but was faithful to his vocation: for when in 1812 his birth and merits induced the emperor to summon him to Milan to enter the guard of honor, he turned from all worldly rank, and as his malady still hung over him, obtained an exemption from the service. The career of arms, even in the service of the Holy See to which he gave his whole heart, never was his object: he never entered it.

He remained at Sinigaglia till Pope Pius VII., in 1814, passed through that city on his return to Rome. Then Mastai hastened to the tomb of St. Peter to resume his studies on the opening of the Ecclesiastical Academy. He arrived in time to witness Rome's rapturous welcome to the holy Pontiff in May, 1814. Soon after his arrival Providence brought the young noble into contact with the director of the Tata Giovanni, a charitable establishment. A single visit filled him with admiration, and from that time young Mastai became so interested in its good works that he consecrated all his leisure to its service.

He was looked for regularly every day by the inmates, but one evening their friend was absent. A cardinal's carriage suddenly reined up at the door to call upon them to run out and aid a young man whom, in the gathering darkness, he discerned lying on the street. Several ran to find their young benefactor writhing in an epileptic fit. He was at once borne into the house, and medical aid summoned.

When he recovered, the young count disappeared for a time. Without announcing his purpose, he made a pilgrimage to the Holy House of Loretto, and there implored the intercession of the Blessed Virgin for his total cure, devoting his health when restored to the service of her divine Son. Then full of hope he continued his theological course under the eminent professor, Joseph Graziosi.

The gradual improvement of his health, and the abating of the attacks of his distressing malady encouraged him greatly, and relying on the hand of God rather than on human skill, he trusted in a complete restoration. To his joy he was admitted at last to minor orders.

His promotion to these holy conditions was followed by actual service in the ministry in 1818. Monsignor Odescalchi, who afterwards laid aside the purple to become a member of the Society of Jesus, was sent in that year, with the venerable Bishop Strambi, to give a mission in the province of Sinigaglia, and he invited the young cleric Mastai to take part in the good work. His first essay in the ministry was thus made under two men whose sanctity is generally revered; indeed the process of the canonization of the venerable Bishop Strambi has already begun.

The labors of the young levite in his humble sphere, discharged with zeal, were crowned with happy results, and he returned invigorated in mind and body, eager to hasten the moment when, as a priest, he might labor for the salvation of souls. He solicited a dispensation to enable him to receive the holy orders of subdeacon and deacon. He was ordained subdeacon in December, 1818, by Monsignor Pietro Caprano, Archbishop of Iconium; and with holy importunity solicited from Pope Pius VII. a further dispensation so that he might receive the priesthood. The Holy Father yielded to his prayer, making it a condition that in celebrating the Holy Sacrifice he should be assisted by another priest. But this condition was a cross to the young priest, who solicited a special audience of the Pope to obtain its removal. Pius VII., as if foreseeing the future, received him with great kindness, and granted his earnest petition, saying:

"Even this favor will we grant you, as I believe that you will never for the future be affected by your disease." Nearly sixty years have elapsed to prove the accuracy of the words of Pope Pius VII.

The noble young deacon accordingly received priestly ordination on the 10th of April, 1819, in the chapel of the ducal palace Doria Pamfili.

A love for the poor and neglected was the great characteristic of the young priest. Instead of seeking preferment or any field for the display of his talents, he had made his home in the Tata Giovanni asylum near the Church of Santa Anna dei Falignami (St. Anne of the Joiners), devoting himself to the care and maintenance of its hundred outcast inmates. The instruction of these forsaken boys in their catechism and their religious duties was his task of predilection. To imprint in the hearts of these boys the truths of religion and guide them to its practice was

PIUS IX.'S FIRST MASS, APRIL 11, 1819.

in his eyes the noblest of duties. The Pope whose utterances in favor of thorough Catholic education have resounded through the world set in his early life an example to all. His conviction of its necessity is based on his own experience as a priest. In the church, or rather chapel, of St. Anne, the young priest said his first mass, on Easter Sunday, in the year 1819, amid the fatherless, to whom he had devoted himself.

This asylum for destitute boys, in its homely name, "Tata Giovanni," recalls its humble and zealous founder, Giovanni Borgi, a poor mason. It was for seven years the residence and especial charge of the zealous priest. The young noble gloried in being permitted to carry on the work begun by the poor and illiterate mason, who, touched with the misery of the homeless and neglected boys, gathered them together to teach them at once to be useful to man and faithful to God. There they are taught the elementary branches, drawing, designing, and other studies to fit them for useful trades. In this institution the plain and homely room once occupied by Pius IX. is still shown, as well as the chair he used while instructing his pupils. On this asylum, which his great patron, Pope Pius VII. had enlarged, the young priest bestowed much of his income, and by wise reforms he increased its power for good, especially in the thoroughness of the inculcating of religious knowledge, and in opening to the inmates higher grades of employment, as engravers, carvers, and sculptors. His own patrimony was used freely for the benefit of those for whom employment could not be found.

Amid all the cares of his later life and his long and eventful pontificate Pius IX. loves to recall those years of obscure devotedness, which had no annalist to record them. He remembers his old pupils. As recently as 1871, a Roman jeweler who was admitted to an audience was complimented by the Pope for his custom of taking apprentices from the Tata Giovanni. "Have you any of my old boys now?" asked his Holiness. The jeweler in vain endeavored to revive his recollections. "You must have such a one," said the Pope, naming one whom he had himself instructed, and learning that he was still in the jeweler's employ, inquired particularly as to his condition, his family, and his life.

The zeal and humility of the young priest were not overlooked. The Vicar of Rome, Cardinal della Genga, noting his ability, resolved to employ him in another field. The revolutions which deprived Spain of most of her transatlantic possessions had in the turmoil of civil war, weakened the religious spirit and desolated the Church. Many sees in Spanish America were deprived of bishops:

churches, missions, and schools were neglected, discipline was relaxed and religious orders were unfruitful of good. The Archdeacon of the Cathedral of Santiago, Joseph Ignatius Cienfuegos, arrived at Rome in 1823, as Ambassador from the Republic of Chili, to request the Holy See to send a delegate apostolic to that republic for the purpose of reorganizing the religious element. Monsignor Muzi, afterwards Bishop of Castello, was selected for this important mission, and consecrated Archbishop of Philippi *in partibus*, and appointed delegate apostolic for Chili and the neighboring states. The Cardinal Vicar, as well as Cardinal Gonsalvi, Secretary of State, urged the zealous priest, Mastai Ferretti, to take part in the mission. The danger of so long a voyage alarmed his mother, who appealed to the Cardinal Secretary of State to recall the appointment, but Pope Pius VII. had already acted upon it, and now wrote to the Countess to assure her of the safe return of her son.

She was not alone in deploring his departure. The young inmates of Tata Giovanni were thunderstruck at the tidings that they were so soon to lose their devoted director. A scene ensued that was never effaced from those young minds. "We knew nothing of the matter," says a worthy shoemaker, then one of the inmates, "we knew nothing, and yet the moment of separation had come. After supper, he did not utter a word. We all noticed it. When grace was ended, we were about to leave the table when he motioned us to sit down. Then he broke the sad news. A cry of real pain ran from one end of the hall to the other. There were a hundred and twenty of us, large and small, and there was not one who was not crying bitterly. Suddenly we all started up to rush to his arms. Some kissed his hands, some grasped his robe, those who could not reach him, called him by every endearing name, as we all implored him not to forsake us. He was himself so touched by our despair, that he began to weep; he pressed the nearest to his heart, saying: 'I would never have believed that our parting would be so sad.' Then he tore himself from us and ran up to his room. He tried to shut the door, but could not: we were all there and made our way in. That night no one went to bed. We all remained in his room, and he spoke words I cannot describe, seeking to calm and comfort us. He urged us to be diligent and obedient to his successor; he told us always to fulfill our duties with joy, and to be ever submissive to the decrees of Providence. Then at daybreak we heard a carriage roll up to the door. It came to tear our benefactor from us. An hour later we were doubly orphans."

Steam had not yet been applied to

the navigation of the seas, and the envoy of the Holy See found no readier way of reaching his destination than to embark at Genoa in a French brig, the Heloise, sailing for Buenos Ayres, and then to travel by land across the continent to Chili. The party, which left Rome July 3, 1823, consisted of Archbishop Muzi, the young priest Mastai Ferretti, the Rev. Mr. Sallusti, secretary, and subsequently historian of the mission, with Archdeacon Cienfuegos and another Chilian priest, Father Raymond Arce, of the order of St. Dominic. Before embarking the Abate Mastai learned to his great grief of the death of Pope Pius VII., his benefactor and friend. Leo XII., however, not only confirmed the powers of his predecessor to the members of the Chilian mission, but in his brief added to Mastai's name the words "who is personally dear to us."

During the delay at Genoa, he was frequently in the society of the archbishop,

Lambruschini, afterwards cardinal, the first meeting of two between whom a conclave was one day to make its choice for the see of Peter.

The Heloise finally sailed on the 5th of May.

A storm soon drove them into the port of Palma, in the island of Majorca, where the envoy of the Holy See and his associates were arrested by the Spanish authorities and subjected to a long interrogatory as to the object of their mission.

The future prisoner of the Vatican was thus confined in a prison by the party of the Revolution. As he remarked to the diplomatic corps in 1870, he then saw the necessity of the independence of the Pope. A ration of food was sent him every day from the vessel, but no letters, papers, or correspondence of any kind.

"On that occasion," says he, "I was initiated in the little devices of close prisoners. We concealed notes in the bread, and I thus learned of the Duke d'Angoulême's victory at Trocadero. After that action, which entailed their ruin, the Spanish insurgents gave no further thought to the poor canon, and we were allowed to depart."

Continuing their voyage, they passed the Straits of Gibraltar, and steered for Teneriffe, thence crossing the Atlantic. Fearful storms beset them all through the voyage, causing much sickness and discomfort. On the 22d of December, the sea broke so violently on the vessel's side as to hurl the young priest across the cabin, and against the partition with great violence. It was deemed almost a miracle that he did not seriously injure Father Arce, who was on his knees in prayer just opposite him.

Towards night Canon Mastai saw the mate, who was throwing the lead, swept off by an enormous wave. He ran out on deck to give the alarm and aid in rescuing him. Various objects were thrown in hopes of giving him support, and a boat was let down, at great risk, which fortunately reached him about two miles from the brig. The storm kept on the following days, but on the 24th lulled somewhat, and Monsignor Muzi said the midnight mass, as Canon Mastai did that at daybreak.

On the second day after the great feast they were in sight of the mouth of the La Plata, only to be driven out to sea again, and it was only on the morning of New Year's day that they anchored before Montevideo, and two days later reached Buenos Ayres.

Here they were received with the greatest joy by the people and clergy, but the government evinced a latent hostility. At that time, owing to the revolutions, South America was almost without bishops, as many had died, and others retired to Spain, while no new nominations had been made, owing to the fact that no arrangements had been entered into between the newly-formed republics and the Holy See. There was an earnest desire to have confirmation conferred by the Prefect Apostolic, and young men long since prepared ordained to the priesthood.

The canon Mastai aided the archbishop in all the labors thus imposed upon him, and conciliated all by his urbanity, zeal, and talents during their brief stay in the city. They left it on the 16th of January, for their long and tedious journey across the Pampas, by the way of Rosario, Cordova, and Mendoza, and then over the Andes. Their route was a constant mission. As the news of their coming spread, the priests prepared their flocks to receive confirmation at the hands of the archbishop sent from Rome by the Holy Father. But if piety thus heralded the progress of the envoys of the Holy See, the tidings reached also the wild Indians of the plains, who at once concluded that so honored a party must possess great wealth. A formidable band of warriors collected to cut them off. Providentially they mistook their time, and arrived too soon at a dangerous pass, and rode off in pursuit only to allow them to escape in safety. But the journey was one of constant alarm and hardship. They were often for days without shelter amid storm and tempest. On the 24th of February, the pious band reached the foot of the Andes, and scaling that great mountain range, the future Pope looked down from its volcanic peaks on the continent unrolled before him. Then descending the rocky mountain side, they reached the rich and luxuriant plains of Chili, and on the 6th of March entered the city of Santiago.

During his whole stay in South America the young priest devoted his time and his talents to the ministry and works of charity, and many a town still points with pride to spots hallowed by the recollection of the great Pope. In one of his journeys across the continent, he found an English officer named Miller, in a wretched pampa inn, tossing in a raging fever. The good priest, allowing his companions to proceed, remained to nurse the stranger, nor did he leave the officer till he was well recovered.

At another time in Chili, he found an aged man dying in a wretched hut amid his large destitute family. The compassionate priest encamped near them, and finding the disease beyond control, remained to instruct and console him. He was rewarded for his care by baptizing the dying man and his whole family. Soon after, this Indian patriarch died in the arms of the noble Italian priest.

He then prepared him for the grave, giving part of his own clothing, and committed his body to the earth with the rites of the Church. After erecting a cross above it, he relieved the wants of the afflicted family, and continued his way loaded with their blessings. So lavish was he in his deeds of charity, that he gave away his whole personal income.

His stay in Chili showed him the difficulties that were to beset religion in the new republics, each of which claimed to succeed to all privileges ever granted by the Holy See to the kings of Spain when those monarchs were regarded as pillars of the Church. Monsignor Muzi, after nearly two years' endeavor to revive religion and perfect the new organization of dioceses, resolved to return. The Chilian government made no provision for the delegation, questioned its powers, and hampered in every way the efforts of Archbishop Muzi. Religious houses had been suppressed, and on every side regular priests driven from their convents were found unable any longer to maintain their community life or follow their rule. To these Archbishop Muzi granted liberty to become secular priests. Even at this the Chilian government took umbrage.

The failure of the mission to restore religious order in Chili augured ill for other parts of Spanish America, but the Prefect Apostolic resolved to make the effort in Peru. The mission embarked at Santiago for Lima in a Chilian schooner. Again storms seemed to pursue them. Their pilot, unfit for his post, was unable to keep the vessel off the rocky shore, and danger menaced all, when the fishing-boat of a worthy man named Bako came to their relief, and piloted them safely into the port of Arica. The next day the canon Mastai visited the humble seaside cabin of his deliverer, and gave him a purse containing four hundred dollars. Nor did he soon forget the service. When raised to the chair of Peter, he sent his portrait and a sum equal to his first gift to Bako. The good fisherman set up the picture to receive all honor: but blessings had come with the first gift. He was well off, and distributed the second gift among the poor in the name of Pope Pius IX.

The envoys of the Holy See found Peru as ill-disposed as Chili had proved. They returned to Chili, and as the Heloise was at Valparaiso, they re-embarked on her, and sailing around Cape Horn, were once more on the ocean way, reaching Genoa on the 5th of June, 1825.

On his return to Rome after his American mission, the priest Mastai Ferretti found that new honors awaited him. His zeal in discharging the duties of his state and of any post committed to him showed that he was destined to serve the Church in many and varied capacities. The experience acquired during his travels and residence in the Spanish American republics was to be of great service in the perplexing questions which were from time to time laid before the Holy See.

He was made canon of the Church of Santa Maria in Via Lata, and in 1825 Pope Leo XII. appointed him president of the commission which directed the hospice of San Michele, a vast establishment in the Trastevere, near the Porta Portese, founded by Pope Innocent X. as a refuge for homeless children. Later Popes enlarged and endowed the institution, adding departments for other objects of charity, so that at this time San Michele was a refuge open to every form of human misery, but at the same time a training school for all mechanical trades, and even a school of fine art.

When Canon Mastai Ferretti assumed the direction this great establishment was in a critical condition. Mismanagement had nearly produced bankruptcy. He reformed the whole operation of the institution, evincing remarkable administrative abilities. Though his sense of justice prompted him to a new and liberal measure, by which the apprentices now receive a part of their earnings, this did not prevent the director from increasing the revenue so as to escape all danger, and place the hospice in a position of ease. "The prudence with which he discharged the laborious functions of that office is yet gratefully remembered by those who were then acquainted with the institution." But it may be added that he used his own resources without stint, remarking: "What is property good for in the hands of a priest, except to be devoted seasonably in the service of charity?"

The humble priest, so devoted to the forsaken young, was left among them for about twenty months, when Pope Leo XII. made the young canon one of his domestic prelates, and resolved to give his abilities a wider field. He preconized

Monsignor John Mary Mastai Ferretti, Archbishop of Spoleto.

The very day of his preconization he went to visit his old friends at the Tata Giovanni, and then withdrew to solitude to prepare for the episcopal consecration, which he received on Whitsunday, 1827, in the Church of San Pietro in Vincoli, from the hands of Cardinal Castiglioni, afterwards Pope Pius VIII. He said his first mass as bishop, as he had his first mass as priest, in the Church of St. Anne, the chapel of his children at Tata Giovanni. He then received the pallium from the hands of the Pope, and addressing a pastoral letter to his flock, set out for his episcopal city.

He was not rich, being only a younger son of a noble but by no means wealthy family: he had held no lucrative preferments, and though a strict and judicious administrator of public trusts, he could not keep aught for himself. He had given to the poor and in good works so freely that he had to sell a little property he owned and borrow money in order to meet the expenses of his installation.

Spoleto, the capital of a province, afforded a wide field for the zeal and energy of the new archbishop. Much was to be done to revive piety amid people whose faith was weakened by revolutionary ideas and secret societies. Soon missions were given in all the parishes, confraternities established, and a new life infused.

In one of his earliest good works we see the influence of the holy work in which he had been so long engaged. He founded a large orphan asylum with a manual labor school to train poor orphans to useful trades, so that they might be above the temptations of want. This establishment was so endowed as to remain a monument of his zeal and love of the poor.

The election of Gregory XVI. in February, 1831, was seized upon by malcontents, who, inspired by the French revolution of the preceding year, now sought to overthrow the existing governments in Italy.

While Archbishop Mastai Ferretti acted the part of a father to his clergy, encouraging the desponding, consoling the unhappy, arousing the torpid, his diocese thus became the scene of one of those popular outbreaks which secret societies have made so frequent in the nineteenth century. Generally a few daring and active men terrorize the quiet, and overthrow established order only to place unscrupulous men in power.

The insurgents of the province, under Sercognarri, were soon routed and scattered by the Austrian troops, and came in full flight to Spoleto to seek a refuge and food. Rebels as they were to the Sovereign Pontiff, the archbishop sought to save them. He went out to the Austrian general who was in pursuit of the fugitive revolutionists, and induced him to halt, promising to disarm them himself. He then proceeded to the camp of the insurgents, and after showing them in the most convincing language the extent of their crime, he induced them to lay down their arms, several thousand muskets, and five pieces of artillery. Money was then distributed among them to meet their immediate wants, but confiding rather in this brave archbishop than in their own leaders, they asked to receive the money directly from his hands.

Two of the Bonaparte family, forgetting the debt of honor they owed to the Papacy, took part in this insurrection. One died while endeavoring to escape through the unhealthy marshes; the other, the future Napoleon III., is said to have avoided a like fate or a dungeon by the aid of the Archbishop of Spoleto.

The insurrection was quelled. It had not been without sympathizers in the city of Spoleto. The zealous chief of the police had pierced the vail of the conspiracy and brought to the archbishop a list of the accomplices. "My worthy sir," exclaimed the archbishop, "you do not understand your profession or mine. When a wolf wishes to devour the sheep he does not warn the shepherd." The list unread and unopened was soon burning before his eyes.

The archbishop had remained at his post amid all the troubles, but the civil authorities of Perugia and Spoleto fled. Cardinal Bernetti, then Secretary of State, at once confided to the archbishop the command of the two provinces. His ability and popularity were evinced by the prompt restoration of order throughout that part of the Papal States.

In January, 1832, another affliction fell upon the province. A desolating earthquake spread misery throughout the district of Spoleto. Wherever the distress was greatest, the good archbishop was found bearing aid and consolation to the homeless, who were endeavoring to erect rude shelters to cover them, and to obtain food and other necessaries of life. His energetic charity, in spite of his own poverty, relieved promptly and efficiently. He sought alms everywhere.

In view of the great virtues and great administrative ability of Archbishop Mastai Ferretti, Pope Gregory XVI., on the 17th of December, 1832, translated him to the more important episcopal see of Imola, which had just been resigned by Cardinal Giustiniani.

Archbishop Mastai Ferretti left Spoleto amid the regrets of his clergy and people. At Imola he was received with joy. He soon showed his wonted energy, and his love for the poor and the outcast. His life seems to have been devoted to the idea that, as modern society degrades, demoralizes, and then rejects these victims, the Church should ever be on the alert to save and restore them to God. He established an orphan home where a number of boys were to be sheltered and instructed, going every day to workshops where, as apprentices, they acquired some useful trade. He called in the Sisters of Charity of Saint Vincent de Paul, and to them committed the care of a conservatory for orphan girls, as well as of an academy and free school, which rendered great service. A hospital and an asylum for the deaf and dumb were established and placed under the direction of the same sisters.

But his care was not confined merely to the bodily wants. He founded a preparatory seminary for students whose limited means prevented them entering the Episcopal Seminary, thus enabling them to pursue their studies and follow their vocation. While he prepared to recruit the ranks of the clergy, he provided for the veterans, by founding a home for aged and infirm priests. For those still laboring in the vineyard, he established a house of retreat, where at stated times, in turn, part of his clergy came to follow the spiritual exercises for several days, that, acquiring new light and strength from silent prayer, they might discharge more effectually their holy mission among their flocks. He also established a system of Conferences on Holy Scripture, with wise regulations, and always presided in person at the meetings.

The condition of the churches of his diocese was not overlooked. He repaired many, restored the episcopal residence, and completed the façade of the cathedral.

It excited no astonishment when it became known that Pope Gregory XVI. intended to raise the good Archbishop of Imola to the purple. He was, in fact, reserved *in petto*, in the consistory of the 23d of December, 1839, and proclaimed cardinal on the 14th of December in the ensuing year. While his duties as a member of the Sacred College, that council of the Pope and Senate of the Church, increased his cares and labors, they did not divert his mind from the wants of his diocese. He established a refuge for female penitents, or as he himself expressed it, a home for "lost daughters of the world soliciting admission into the fold of Jesus." From his own private means he purchased a suitable building and fitted it for their reception. For its direction he selected the Sisters of our Lady of the Good Shepherd, and in 1845, obtained a colony of that community from the mother-house at Angers, in France.

As bishop and cardinal, his habit of life was extremely simple; his income was expended almost entirely in good works, so that his constant charities often left him without means. On one occasion a poor woman applied to him for alms, and her distress was so evident that he wished to relieve her; but he searched in vain for any money. Taking a silver dish from his table, he told her to pawn it at the Mount of Piety, and obtain means to relieve her wants. "I can at any time redeem it," said the good cardinal. His attendant soon missing the article, made search in vain, and came to report that it had been stolen; the cardinal's confusion betrayed his secret, and his attendant knew by experience that the piece of plate had been sacrificed at the call of charity.

Nor is this the only incident of the kind related. In the February following, an event occurred, in which his zeal and courage were displayed. Just as the shades of night were gathering over the city, the Cardinal, as was his habitual practice, entered his cathedral to pay a visit to our Lord in the Blessed Sacrament. The holy calm of the hour and the place were suddenly broken by the sacristan, who rushed towards the cardinal imploring him to hasten for God's sake, as they were murdering a man in the sacristy.

He knew his archbishop well, when he thus summoned him to the midst of danger, and did not urge him to provide for his own safety. The cardinal hastening to the vestry, found a youth of twenty stretched on a bench, bleeding from a dangerous bayonet wound. He had fled to the church for protection and sank there. Scarcely had Cardinal Mastai reached his side when three armed men burst in, still thirsting for their victim's blood. The cardinal confronted the armed ruffians, and presenting his pectoral cross, commanded them to retire. Hardened as they were, they quailed before the decisive mien and the holy fire that lighted up the gentle face of the cardinal bishop. They slunk away, leaving him to minister to their victim, and rally the fast-vanishing vital strength.

In the early part of June, 1846, while Cardinal Mastai was making a spiritual retreat with many of his priests, he received the announcement of the death of Pope Gregory XVI. He returned to his episcopal residence, and after offering up a solemn requiem for the repose of the soul of the late sovereign Pontiff, repaired to Rome. He entered the capital of the Christian world on the 12th of June, and two days afterwards he, with the other members of the Sacred College of Cardinals, entered the Conclave, or Assembly for the election of a sovereign Pontiff.

THE ARMS OF POPE PIUS IX.

CHAPTER II.

THE ELECTION.—CARDINAL MASTAI FERRETTI CHOSEN POPE.—THE ORDINANCE OF AMNESTY. — THE MEMORANDUM OF 1831.— POPULARITY OF PIUS IX. AT HOME AND ABROAD.—OPINIONS OF AMERICAN STATESMEN AS TO THE POPE.

THE election of a sovereign Pontiff has excited the wonder of those who study the perplexed systems of human institutions. The whole course is so free from all that can hamper the cardinals in their perfect freedom of action. The choice is so fully their own that even in this men should discern the overruling hand of God.

From all parts to which the tidings of the late Pope's death have reached, the cardinals come to Rome. The people and the clergy watch with interest these venerable men; many advanced in years, illustrious for long services rendered to the Church, holy bishops, learned doctors, able in council or in government. One of them will remain in Rome as sovereign Pontiff, the rest resume their accustomed duties.

It is vain to attempt to pierce the secrets of the future, or decide on whom the choice will ultimately fall. But the pious look for some outward manifestation of the divine will. As the carriage of Cardinal Mastai Ferretti passed through Fossombrone, an episcopal city in the delegation of Urbino and Pesaro, the faithful gathered around to scrutinize the face of the occupant, when a white dove sailing through the air alighted on the carriage. At once the cry arose: " Evviva! evviva! behold the Pope! " But thoughts of his elevation could scarcely have entered the mind of one so young and so recently raised to the cardinalate.

The course of the election is simple, and as thoughtful Protestant writers have admitted, better calculated than any other the world has ever seen to secure the real free choice of those electing. When a Pope expires the cardinal camerlingo, with the apostolic notaries and attendants, attests the fact, and the seal of the fisherman, the official seal used by the Pope, is broken. The body of the deceased pontiff then lies in state in St. Peter's, for nine days, when after a solemn mass of requiem it is deposited in a temporary tomb.

The next day the cardinals in Rome assemble in St. Peter's, and after a solemn mass to invoke the guidance of the Holy Ghost, they enter the Conclave. For centuries the Conclave or Assembly of Cardinals to elect a Pope has been held in the Quirinal palace. Here in different apartments after the death of Pope Gregory XVI. fifty-four cardinals and their attendants were lodged, on Sunday, June 14,

1846. The bulls regulating the election of a sovereign Pontiff were read, and all the cardinals swore to observe them. All windows opening from without and all entrances except one were then walled up, and that one had two locks—one inside and one without. This door is opened only to allow any cardinal who falls sick to retire: or to admit any who arrive at a later day. A small window allows the approach of the ambassadors of France, Spain, and Austria, who have each claimed the right to object to one proposed cardinal.

Meanwhile masses were constantly offered, the Blessed Sacrament was exposed in the churches, and visited by the confraternities, clergy, and people, all praying fervently to God to direct the choice of the cardinals.

Every day—morning at six o'clock and afternoon at two—the cardinals assembled in the chapel for the scrutiny. In the middle of the Pauline chapel stood two chalices to receive the votes. Each ballot is written and folded in a prescribed form, and each cardinal as he deposited it read the oath prescribed: "I call to witness God who will be my judge, that I choose the person before God, whom I judge ought to be elected, and that I will do the same in acceding." Cardinal Prince Altieri first proposed the name of Cardinal Mastai Ferretti, and the scrutiny of the first ballots showed that he had received more votes than any other. But two-thirds of the whole number of living cardinals are required for a choice. The voting went on. At each scrutiny the votes in his favor increased, and on Monday it became evident that the choice of the Sacred College would center on him. The prospect filled him with alarm, and he spent the night in prayer, begging God to avert the burden from him.

The next morning he was appointed to

open the ballots. As he did so he saw his own name on almost every paper that he unfolded. He could not complete the task. In a voice broken by emotion, he exclaimed: "Brethren, spare me, take pity on my weakness, I am unworthy." The scrutiny completed at last showed that he had received the requisite number of votes. A Pope had been elected before a single ambassador, notified by his sovereign, had approached the window.

The scrutators declared his name, the master of ceremonies and the secretary summoned by the junior cardinal deacon entered. Cardinal Mastai knelt to adore God who had brought him face to face with an awful responsibility for His own glory. The cardinals, a moment before his equals, withdrew, leaving him alone with God. When he arose, Cardinal Macchi, the subdean, with two others, advanced before him and asked whether he accepted the election. Deeply moved, the newly elected Pope answered that he submitted to the will of God. Then the baldachinos were taken down from above the seats of all the other cardinals, and the cardinals who had sat on either side of him withdrew. When Cardinal Macchi asked him what name he intended to take, the words "Pius IX." were uttered for the first time.

Two cardinal deacons then conducted him behind the high altar, where he assumed the pontifical habit, and then in front of the altar he received the homage of the cardinals, and the ring of the fisherman was placed on his hand.

After this the first cardinal deacon, while the choir sang *Ecce sacerdos magnus*, went out on the balcony over the entrance to the palace and proclaimed the election to the people, who had already gathered there. "I announce to you a great joy," he said. "We have as Pope the most eminent and the most Reverend John

Mary, Cardinal of the Roman Church, Mastai Ferretti, who has taken the name of Pius IX."

Loud shouts of joy rose up from the people, the cannon of the castle of St. Angelo thundered forth, the bells of Rome rang out a peal of joy, and a general holiday ensued.

As the cardinals advanced on the balcony, leaving an open space, the people all looked up to see the scarcely known Bishop of Imola. The mild and benignant countenance won all hearts: and when with streaming eyes he lifted up his hands to heaven, and then extended them in benediction over his people, the cry went up: "We have a Pope, he loves us! he is our father!" He announced his elevation to his brothers in Sinigaglia in these modest words:

"ROME, June 16, at ¾ past 11, P. M.
"The Blessed God, who humbles and

exalts, has been pleased to raise me from insignificance to the most sublime dignity on earth. May His holy will be ever done. I am sensible to a certain extent of the immense weight of such a charge, and I also feel my utter incapacity, not to say, the entire nullity of my powers. Cause prayers to be offered, and do you also pray for me. The conclave has lasted forty-eight hours. If the city should wish to make any public demonstration on the occasion, I request that you will take measures—indeed I desire it—that the whole sum so destined be applied to purposes which may be judged useful to the city, by the chief magistrate and the council. As to yourselves, my dear brothers, I embrace you with all my heart in Jesus Christ: and far from exulting, take pity on your brother, who gives you all his apostolic blessing."

On Sunday, June 21st, 1846, he was

borne to St. Peter's, where the chapter received him at the door, singing *Tu es Petrus*. After kneeling in prayer before the altar of the Blessed Sacrament, he received the homage of the cardinals beneath the chair of Saint Peter, whose successor he is. Then he assumed the pontifical vestments, and he moved in procession around the choir of the mighty basilica, till he reached the chapel of St. Processus and St. Martinianus, where the master of ceremonies lighted a bunch of flax, saying: " Holy Father, thus passeth the glory of the world." On his return to the altar mass began. During it a cardinal descended to the tomb of the apostles, and intoned an ancient litany, which seemed to be the prayer of all the past ages of Christendom welling up from the grave to heaven. After the mass the Pope received the insignia of Pontiff and King.

The triple crown was placed on his

SAINT PETER'S CHAIR AT ROME.

head in the Loggia of the Vatican by the first cardinal deacon.

Pius IX. began his wonderful reign, which was to be unexampled in length, remarkable in the great acts performed, in the great sufferings undergone.

His first acts showed his love of his people. Dowries for poor girls were distributed in all the churches of Rome and the vicinity; liberal alms were given to the poor, the tools and necessary objects which poverty had forced many to pawn at the "Pious Mounts," those loan offices of Catholic Rome, were redeemed and restored; the obligations of poor debtors in the prisons were paid.

The government of his states was now his concern. Summoned thus suddenly to grasp the reins of power, his policy was to be adopted and laid out. His heart prompted him to adopt the mild and gentle course which had proved successful in his brief civil authority at Spoleto. Many

Romans implicated in revolutionary attempts were in exile. He resolved to begin by an amnesty that would permit these to return, and he trusted to win all by a wise and moderate administration.

A month after his elevation, he issued, July 16, 1846, an ordinance of amnesty. This remarkable document, the glorious initiatory of the political acts of Pope Pius IX., remitted the remainder of the term of punishment of all in prison for political offenses, with no condition except that of a solemn declaration in writing on their honor, that they would not abuse the favor, and that they would in future live as dutiful subjects.

Those in exile, through their own choice, or by legal sentence, were to be admitted to pardon within a year, by applying to a papal nuncio.

All who were under the supervision of the police, or already indicted, were relieved at once from further prosecution. Of all indeed who had been guilty of practices against the state, none were excepted from the amnesty except thirty-nine, ecclesiastics or persons who had held civil or military office, and even for these the path of reparation was thrown open.

This was but one step in his course to gain the goodwill of his people, and to disarm all pretext of discontent. He personally inquired into and improved the administration of the public departments; he rigorously examined into the management of hospitals, prisons, and religious institutions, and enforced needed reforms; he punished fraud and extortion with great severity; he promoted industry by public works and by special rewards; he introduced reforms into the revenue and treasury departments; he remitted some taxes and diminished others; he authorized the establishment of railroads and the introduction of gas for lighting the cities; he appointed laymen to numbers of offices not previously open to them, and gave a wide freedom to the press, reserving only a moderate censorship.

All these reforms he crowned by proposing, in April, 1847, the establishment of a council composed of delegates from the various provinces, a senate whom he might consult and advise as to the best measures for the good of the people.

The course of the Pope found many opponents. Among the cardinals and others long connected with the government, habituated to other principles, these steps were regarded as highly dangerous and sure to lead to disastrous results.

A few years previous, in 1831, several of the European powers had deemed it not unwise to interfere in the government of the Papal States. The schismatical Greek emperor of Russia, the Protestant kings of England and Prussia, seconded by the Catholic Emperor of Austria, and king of France, had laid before the Pope a programme of reforms which they advised, a programme drawn up not by an Italian who might know the real wants of the case, but by a fanatical German Protestant.

Now Pius IX., fully aware of the condition of his States, entered on the path of reform, and a general alarm ensued. Austria, one of the very powers to the Memorandum of 1831, now saw danger to her Italian power in the course of Pius IX. France seems to have measured the dynasty of Orleans by the Pontificate of Gregory XVI., and now rejected Louis Philippe; Protestant and Greek alike beheld with chagrin rational liberty established in the Roman States. Not one of them cordially supported the Pope.

The revolutionary party beheld his course with dismay. Pius IX. was removing every pretext for their plots and conspiracies. They saw with alarm their old dupes promising devotion to Pius IX.: they saw, too, that open opposition would then be fruitless. They attempted by flattery and by promises to make him the tool of their anti-Christian war.

Pius IX. was daily winning the hearts of the people. He went through Rome on foot with a small retinue. One day, while on his way from the Quirinal to the chapel of a Visitation convent where he was to say mass, a little boy ran up and asked him: "Are you the Pope?" "Yes, my little friend, I am." "I have no father," said the boy. "I will be a father to you," said the Pope, who, finding the child to be really an orphan, proved really a father, educating and providing for him.

Children had always seen in him a friend and protector. On one occasion, the Pope heard some confusion among the

Swiss guards, and ascertained that a boy was trying to push his way through them in order to present a petition to the Pope. The little fellow's appeal was soon in the hands of the sovereign Pontiff. In the language of his age, the boy told of his struggling widowed mother, and of a hard-hearted landlord who was about to evict them; with the simplicity of a child, he asked the Pope to lend him four dollars to save his mother from being put into the street, promising to repay it when he was old enough to earn money. The kind-hearted Pope told him to return the next day, and having by inquiry ascertained that little Paul's story was true, gave him, when he reappeared, ten dollars for his mother. The honest little fellow returned six, saying he had not asked for so much. "Take them again, my good boy," said the Pope, "and tell your mother that I will look after her for the future."

No ruler ever did more to endear himself to his people, or to assure them the best of governments. All that the great powers had advised was granted, and more. All that the better class of citizens had ever desired was established. Open opposition was at first more than the crafty statesman or the infidel revolutionist, both equally stimulated by hatred of the Church, durst venture upon. The world rang plaudits on the course of the liberal Pope. Meetings were held in many parts to express sympathy with Pius IX. To one held in New York city, where the "Popular Hymn of Pius IX.," by Rossini, was sung enthusiastically, Martin Van Buren, ex-President of the United States, wrote: "The position recently taken by Pope Pius, and which has been hitherto so nobly sustained by the people of Italy, has not only been in the highest degree patriotic, but, what is scarcely less important, been sustained by a steady hand." "Regarded only as the political head of a State, laboring in behalf of the enfranchisement and consequent happiness of the people, the sovereign Pontiff justly claims the best wishes, the hearty cheers, and all proper co-operation of the friends of reform, in whatever country they may reside, or to whatever sect or class they may belong." Words which, coming from one who had himself been the elected head of a great nation, deserve to be remembered in view of subsequent events.

James Buchanan, who was to hold the same lofty position, wrote:

"I have watched with intense anxiety the movements of Pius IX., in the difficult and dangerous circumstances by which he is surrounded, and, in my opinion, they have been marked with consummate wisdom and prudence. Firm without being rash, liberal without proceeding to such extremes as might endanger the success of his glorious mission, he seems to be an instrument destined by Providence to accomplish the political regeneration of his country."

Similar opinions were expressed by Samuel J. Tilden, elected also to the presidency in more recent times. "It is related," said he, "of the truly illustrious ruler whom we are here to honor, that, laying his hand upon the New Testament, 'My people,' said he, 'may expect justice and mercy from me, for my only guide is this book.' The fruits of this enlightened resolution are those reforms of institutions and administration which have filled Italy with gladness." "Difference of religious faith shall not restrain me from rendering the homage of just applause to acts so beneficent, to an example so valuable in the extent as well as the nature of its influence; so appropriate to a man who is at once a religious and a civil chief: and so worthy of the head of a venerable Church, in whose bosom was preserved, during the long, dark period when letters and the arts were lost, the germs of religious truth and representative government."

CHAPTER III.

Pius IX. and the Church at Large.—His First Encyclical.—Promotion of Cardinals.—The Pope in the Pulpit.—Ecclesiastical Reforms. — Ireland. — America.— Religious Orders.

We have dwelt upon the early acts of Pope Pius IX. in the government of the States which had for so many centuries been under the sway of the sovereign Pontiffs, and had thus enjoyed freedom and peace, while all around were suffering under tyranny and oppression. But though the whole world applauded the civil reforms, the luster of his Pontificate comes from his higher quality as head of the universal Church.

As a bishop devoted to his flock, with experience in two different dioceses, knowing by personal inspection the wants of the Church in transatlantic countries as well as in Europe, Pius IX. brought to the sovereign Pontificate this experience, with deep personal piety, intense zeal, and a vigilance and love of discipline which were destined to revive a spirit of devotion throughout the Church in times when faith, hope, and charity alike seemed to be growing cold.

His first great act, as head of the Church, addressed to the Catholic hierarchy throughout the world, and through them to the clergy and faithful of every race and clime, was his Encyclical Letter of November 9th, 1846. It was the first of a long series of similar documents which, by their unction, their piety, and their firmness in the cause of religion and order, for more than a quarter of a century stimulated the zeal and devotion of Catholics.

After announcing his unexpected elevation and the despondency that would have overwhelmed him had he not placed his hope in God his salvation, he expresses his consolation in having the bishops as companions and coadjutors. He addresses them to inflame their piety, that, with even more than their wonted alacrity, vigilance, and earnestness, they should keep the night watch over their flocks, and combat with fortitude and constancy the enemy of souls.

He called attention to the fierce and implacable war waged on Catholicity by concerted action, seeking to quench the light of faith in the minds of men, as well as to corrupt their hearts. To accomplish this, some extolled human reason at the expense of Christ's most holy faith, as though faith and reason, flowing from one and the same fountain of immutable and eternal truth, could disagree. Others claimed to subject the Word of God to their own reason, as though he had not constituted a living authority to expound and define it. The sovereign Pontiff then earnestly appeals to their eminent piety to exert themselves with all solicitude and zeal, in exhorting the faithful not to suffer themselves to be led away under any specious pretexts of human progress.

He warns them against the secret societies condemned by so many sovereign Pontiffs, and to the religious indifference so constantly inculcated; against the perverse theories of education, the flood of bad books and periodicals, depraving men and banishing from their hearts all religious influences.

To counteract all these evils, he urges the bishops to encourage fidelity to the Church, not to desist preaching the Word of God, and to labor to form a clergy

CHURCH OF SAINT JOHN LATERAN, ROME.

whose gravity of manners, integrity of life, holiness, and learning may shine forth, accomplishing this by great care in their training and in their selection, as well as by frequent retreats after they are admitted to the priesthood.

Commending himself to their earnest prayers, and the intercession of the Blessed Virgin Immaculate and all the saints, the pious Pontiff imparted to the bishops, and the clergy and faithful committed to their charge, his apostolic benediction.

In order to unite the world in prayer in the difficulties which he well saw the Church must soon experience in its head and its members, the Pope soon after, by Apostolic Letters of the 22d of November, proclaimed an indulgence in form of a Jubilee to all who visited, with the usual conditions of confession and communion and prayers for the intention of the sovereign Pontiff, the churches of St. Peter's, St. John Lateran, and St. Mary Major, or, in places remote from the holy city, three churches appointed by the bishop of the diocese.

In his first promotion of cardinals at the consistory held on the 21st of December, 1846, he admitted to the Sacred College Cajetan Baluffi, his successor in the see of Imola, and Peter Marini, of the order of deacons, reserving *in petto* two others, Joseph Pecci, Bishop of Gubbio, and Joseph Bofondi, whose nomination was published in the following June. In this latter month his second promotion of cardinals added to the Sacred College James Antonelli, of the order of deacons, eminent for his services as minister of finance and prime minister of Pius IX.; James M. A. C. Du Pont, Archbishop of Bourges; Peter Giraud, Archbishop of Cambray, and Charles Vizardelli.

The encyclical aroused the zeal of the bishops to encourage the secular clergy in their respective dioceses to consider seriously the ministry which they had received from God, in order to fulfill its obligations exactly, as well as to train up, by careful schooling of the mind and heart, the young aspirants to the priesthood, that, imbued with sacred sciences, the tradition of the Church, and the doctrines of the holy fathers, they might, in due season, cultivate the vineyard of the Lord and fight his battles. There was still another object of his care: the great family of the religious orders, bodies created in seasons of the Church's want and trial, for the sanctification of the members, and to afford the secular clergy aid in their ministry. These bodies, where true to their institute, had rendered incalculable service, and the number of saints which they had produced from age to age showed how the Spirit of God was among them; but while in their fervor they were thus a consolation to the Church, on the contrary, where relaxation, tepidity, and worldliness crept in, these orders became a source of scandal to the faithful, and an object of reproach and triumph for the enemies of the Church. Hence one great object of Pius IX., on his accession, was to revive the true spirit in the various religious orders.

The city of Rome soon felt that the sovereign Pontiff was full of zeal and energy, in reforming abuses, in encouraging the bishops and clergy, and in setting an example. As he moved through Rome, his heart was afflicted at the increasing profanity among working men, and their evident neglect of the laws of the Church in regard to fasting and abstinence. One day he reproached the celebrated pulpit orator, Father Ventura, with neglecting to instruct the people on these points in his discourses. The great preacher declared that he had often made them the theme of his discourses, but that his words seemed to fall unheeded. "I would gladly make the attempt myself," said Pius IX., "but it is so long since a Pope has appeared in the pulpit, that I fear I shall not be more successful." "Your Holiness is mistaken," said Father Ventura; "the attachment of the people to your person is a guarantee that your words will be heard with the deepest attention." "You have decided it. I see that you are to preach on the last day of the octave of Epiphany, at the church of San Andrea della Valle. Let me take your place, but keep the matter a secret."

On that day, January 13, 1847, Rome witnessed a spectacle not seen since the days of St. Gregory VII. A congregation gathered in the afternoon to listen to the words of the popular preacher, when to their wonder and their joy they beheld the Pope himself advance to the strada, which is the pulpit in Italian churches. The impulsive hearts gave vent to exclamations of surprise and joy. When silence was restored, he addressed them:

"I cannot, without lively emotion, my beloved children, recall the tokens of love which you came to offer me on the first day of the year. My heart thanked you for your felicitations, and referring, as I justly should, to the honor of God, what you do for me, his unworthy vicar, I invited you to bless the name of our Lord in these words, 'Blessed be the name of the Lord.' You all replied with an accent of faith, 'Now and forever.' I remind you of this solemn engagement, for there are men in this city, the center of Catholicity, men, few indeed in number, who profane the holy name of God by blasphemy. Do you all who are here at present receive this mission from me: Proclaim everywhere that I expect nothing from these men. They hurl against heaven the stone which will crush them in its fall. It is heaping up the measure of ingratitude to blaspheme the name of the common Father, who gives us life, and with life, all the blessings we enjoy. Tell those of my children who offend him by such outrages no longer to give such scandal in the holy city. I wish also to speak to you of the precept of fasting. A great many parents have told me of the sufferings they experience in beholding the demon of impurity exercise his ravages among the young men. Our Lord himself tells us in the gospel that by prayer and fasting is this devastating demon chained, who goes ravaging the earth, and who not only poisons the sources of the life of individuals, families, and all society, but who especially consummates the ruin of immortal souls. After these two counsels, it remains for me to pray to God to bless you all: Lord, look down from heaven; turn toward us thy quickening glance. Visit this vineyard which thy right hand hath planted.

It is thine, O Lord; thou hast watered it with thy blood; thou hast preserved it. Visit it, not to punish the wicked, but to make them feel the sweet effects of thy mercy. Visit it to heal the wound of incredulity which devours the world. Visit it, and visiting it remove that iron hand which weighs so heavily on it. Pour into the hearts of the rising generation those two dearest attributes of youth, modesty and docility. Extinguish those fatal animosities which divide citizens and array them against each other. Visit it, O Lord, and visiting it warn the sentinels of Israel to give good example and arm themselves with divine strength and prudence to watch over the interests of the people committed to their care. Vouchsafe, O my God, to hear my prayer, and pour forth on this people, on this city, and on the whole world, thy sweetest benedictions!"

Pope Pius IX. showed his interest in the

Church in the United States by approving, on the 7th of February, 1847, the decrees of the Sixth Provincial Council of Baltimore, and by the erection of new sees at Albany, Buffalo, Cleveland, and Galveston.

To obviate the objections raised by unscrupulous men he modified the ancient episcopal oath so as to remove even the shadow of an objection. In a letter issued some months later to Archbishop Eccleston, the sovereign Pontiff says to him and the bishops of the United States: "We are greatly rejoiced at the cheering testimony you have sent us of the very great and rapid increase of the Catholic religion in the United States. We warmly congratulate you on your virtue and labors. We freely promise you that nothing will be omitted on our part that can aid you, or be useful to the cause of the Church over which you preside."

The fatherly heart of Pius IX. was moved by the terrible accounts of the famine which desolated Ireland, attended by a dread pestilence. He ordered prayers to be offered in behalf of the sufferers, and urged the clergy and people of his own States as well as all who were visiting Rome from piety or curiosity to join in relieving a land so terribly afflicted. Large amounts were thus forwarded to the hierarchy in Ireland to distribute where the need was sorest. As the misery continued, he issued on the 25th of March, 1847, an encyclical letter, addressed to all patriarchs, primates, archbishops, and bishops, granting a plenary indulgence to all who united in prayer for three days for the afflicted kingdom, and approaching the sacraments, assisted the people of Ireland by the gifts of charity. He urged the prelates to stimulate the zeal of their people in alms-giving. "What effort ought we not make," says the great Pope, "to raise up that nation now suffering under such a disaster, when we know how great the fidelity of the clergy and people of Ireland is and always has been toward the Apostolic See; how in the most dangerous times their firmness in the profession of the Catholic religion has been conspicuous; by what labors the clergy of Ireland have toiled for the propagation of the Catholic religion in the remotest regions of the world!"

The appeal did not fall unheeded. At the call of the Vicar of Christ prayers and alms were offered up in all parts for the suffering poor in Ireland. The death of the great Liberator, Daniel O'Connell, while on his way to Rome, and the arrival of his great heart in that city, where it was his wish that it should rest, tended also to deepen the interest in Ireland. On giving audience to the son of the deceased, Pius IX. pronounced a eulogy on Daniel O'Connell, and said: "Since I have been denied the happiness, so long desired, of embracing the hero of Christendom, let me at least have the consolation of embracing his son," and at the same time the Holy Father pressed him twice to his heart.

Ireland and America were not alone in his thoughts. The position of the Catholics in Switzerland, Russia, and throughout the world engaged his attention.

To carry out his views in regard to the religious orders, he issued on the 17th of June, 1847, an encyclical, addressed to the heads of all the religious orders in the Church, urging them to renewed efforts for the restoration of their rules with primitive fervor. He established a special congregation of cardinals to consider the condition of the religious orders. To those in Rome he gave his personal attention in a way that soon convinced members of the religious orders that the Pope was serious in his great work. One evening, at a late hour, Pius IX. appeared at the door of a convent in Rome. The porter answered the summons gruffly and told the visitor that all were asleep, and that he must come the next day. When he recognized the white soutane of the Pope he was all confusion and opened in haste. The Pope inspected the convent and ordered the roll of the community to be called. Two were found to be absent. On the pretext of the heat of the weather they had been allowed to go into the city to sleep. The Pope censured the prior for thus conniving at laxity of discipline, and the next day ordered the two religious to expiate their fault in a house of ecclesiastical correction.

Under the impulse thus given, a new fervor arose in all the religious bodies.

In an allocution to the cardinals on the Consistory of the 17th of December, 1847, Pius IX. congratulated the sacred college on the renewal of a cordial understanding with Spain, by means of which he had been enabled to appoint a number of bishops in that country once so devoted to the Church. He alluded too to the favorable appearance of the Catholic cause in Russia, and repudiated certain theories ascribed to him. Against religious indifferentism so zealously advocated in our days, and made as it were a state creed, he said : " It is assuredly not unknown to you, venerable brethren, that in our times many of the enemies of the Catholic faith especially direct their efforts toward placing every monstrous opinion on the same level with the doctrine of Christ, or of confounding it therewith, and so they try more and more to propagate that impious system of the indifference of religions. But quite recently, we shudder to say it, men have appeared who have thrown such reproaches upon our name and apostolic dignity, that they do not hesitate to slander us, as if we shared in their folly and favored the aforesaid most wicked system. From the measures, in no wise incompatible with the sanctity of the

Catholic religion, which, in certain affairs relating to the civil government of the Pontifical States, we thought fit in kindness to adopt, as tending to the public advantage and prosperity, and from the amnesty graciously bestowed upon some of the subjects of the same States at the beginning of our pontificate, it appears that these men have desired to infer that we think so benevolently concerning every class of mankind, as to suppose that not only the sons of the Church, but that the rest also, however alienated from Catholic unity they may remain, are alike in the way of salvation, and may arrive at everlasting life.

"We are at a loss from horror to find words to express our detestation of this new and atrocious injustice that is done us. We do indeed love all mankind with the inmost affection of our heart, yet not otherwise than in the love of God, and of our Lord Jesus Christ, who came to seek and to save that which had perished, who died for all, who wills all men to be saved, and to come to the knowledge of the truth; who therefore sent his disciples into the whole world to preach the gospel to every creature, proclaiming that they who should believe and be baptized should be saved, but they who should believe not should be condemned; who therefore will be saved let them come to the pillar and ground of faith, which is the Church; let them come to the true Church of Christ, which in its bishops and in the Roman Pontiff, the chief head of all, has the succession of apostolical authority, never at any time interrupted; which has never counted aught of greater moment than to preach and by all means to keep and defend the doctrine proclaimed by the apostles, by Christ's command; which, from the apostles' time downward, has increased in the midst of difficulties of every kind; and being illustrious through-

GENERAL VIEW OF ROME AND OF THE CASTLE OF SAINT ANGELO.

out the whole world by the splendor of miracles, multiplied by the blood of martyrs, exalted by the virtues of confessors and virgins, strengthened by the most wise testimonies of the fathers, hath flourished and doth flourish in all the regions of the earth, and shines refulgent in the perfect unity of the faith, of sacraments, and of holy discipline."

CHAPTER IV.

The Civil Affairs of Rome.—Italy in a Ferment.—The Fundamental Statute.—The Italian War against Austria.—Defeat of Charles Albert.—Change of Ministry.—Violence of the Revolutionists against the Pope.—The Church in Russia.—Spain.—France.

The position of Pius IX. as a sovereign at last became critical. The vast combination against authority and against Catholic truth was then in full operation throughout Europe. The Catholic Swiss formed the Sonderbund, to save, if possible, their ancient religious liberty; elsewhere the revolutionary party sought the overthrow of existing governments. In Italy, and especially at Rome, these men, after pledging their words at the time of the amnesty, were plotting to destroy alike the temporal power of the Holy See, and the Church. Mazzini and his accomplices had, while praising the liberal concessions of Pius IX. to the popular feeling, stimulated the masses to new and exorbitant demands.

Almost simultaneously an insurrection at Palermo spread over the kingdom of the two Sicilies, and extorted from the king a constitution; Austria and Prussia were convulsed by similar movements. In France the Revolution rose against its own work, and weary of the constitutional monarchy established in 1830, now rejected the house of Orleans, as it then rejected the elder branch of Bourbon, and proclaimed a republic.

On the 10th of February Pope Pius IX., in an address, said: "Romans! The Pontiff who for two years has received from you so many proofs of love and fidelity is deaf neither to your desire nor your fear. It is our constant thought how to develop and perfect, without infringing on what we owe the Church, those civil institutions which we have created, not impelled by force, but yielding only to our desire to benefit our people. Before the public voice sought it, we had planned a reorganization of the militia. To enlarge the sphere of action for all whose ability and experience might benefit the state we have increased the number of laymen in our Council of State. If the concord of sovereigns to whom Italy owes the recent reforms is the guarantee of the preservation of these advantages, we have cultivated this harmony by preserving and strengthening the most friendly relations with them. Nothing in fine that can contribute to the tranquillity and dignity of the state shall be neglected, Romans and pontifical subjects, by your father and sovereign, who has given you the most unmistakable proofs of his solicitude, and who stands ready to give you still more, if God only vouchsafes to grant to his prayers the grace to behold your hearts and those of all Italians inspired by the true spirit of his wisdom. But on the other hand, he is ready to resist, resting on the very strength of the institutions already granted, all disorderly movements, in like manner as he would resist demands repugnant to his duty and your happiness."

On convoking the officers of the civic guard, he found that he could not rely on that force to maintain order or to suppress any rising of the anarchists. Events came hurrying on. Prince Corsini, a senator, with the members of the municipality of

Rome, sought an audience to demand the establishment of a representative government. The Pope's reply was clear: "Everybody knows that I have been incessantly engaged in giving the government the form claimed by those gentlemen and required by the people. But everybody must understand the difficulty encountered by him who unites two supreme dignities. What can be effected in one night in a secular state cannot be accomplished without mature examination at Rome, in consequence of the necessity to fix a line of separation between the two powers. Nevertheless, I hope that in a few days the constitution will be ready and that I shall be able to proclaim a new form of government, calculated to satisfy the people, and more particularly the Senate and the Council, who know better the state of affairs and the situation of the country. May the Almighty bless my desires and labors! If religion derives any advantage therefrom, I will throw myself at the feet of the crucified Jesus, to thank him for the events accomplished by his will, and I will be better satisfied as Chief of the Universal Church than as a temporal prince, if they turn to the greater glory of God."

Herein lay the great difficulty. To many who did not stop to weigh it the separation seemed simple. Many, truly Catholic in heart, thought that if the Pope ceased to be a prince, he would gain as Supreme Pontiff. The result has shown that the Pope, unless an independent prince, cannot be free: if any other ruler has power in his state or city, the government will attempt to control religion, prevent the existence of religious orders, colleges, seminaries, and libraries, or assume control, and direct them and their property. The missions of the Church throughout the world may be at the mercy of the fickle will of some inconsiderable or inconsiderate power. Such a state may by law bind itself to leave the Pope and the Church entire freedom, but it can repeal and alter its own laws, and alone expounds them.

The movement in the Papal States was ostensibly one to obtain for the people a greater share in the government. It professed to entertain no hostility to religion, but the mask fell at once. The cry was at once raised against the priests, and the expulsion of the Jesuits was demanded, and so fierce became the opposition to that order, that on the 30th of March Pius IX. yielded, and the General of the Society of Jesus prepared to withdraw from the city which still acknowledged the Pope as prince. The point was clear and patent; the people of the Papal States claimed not only self-government, but the right to govern the Church throughout the world, by assuming to decide what religious, if any, it should have, and what ecclesiastical advisers the Head of the Church should have near his person.

The Fundamental Statute, issued by Pope Pius IX., gave his States a constitution. By this the College of Cardinals remained the Senate; a high council and council of deputies were established, to be convoked, prorogued, or dissolved by the sovereign Pontiff. Laws passed by them were to be considered by him in a secret consistory of the cardinals. The Parliament was to introduce no law on ecclesiastical or mixed matters, or contrary to the canons and discipline of the Church, or in contravention of the Fundamental Statute. In the annual budget six hundred thousand scudi were reserved annually for the support of the Holy See, the Sacred College, the Congregations, the Propaganda, and the Diplomatic Corps. All relating to intercourse with foreign powers was reserved to the Pope.

Under this Fundamental Statute the

Parliament met on the 5th of June, Cardinal Altieri reading the message of his Holiness. The two Chambers contained some sincere patriots devoted to their country, their sovereign, and their religion; but it was evident that they were powerless in the hands of the more active partisans of the secret societies who sought the overthrow of all existing institutions.

The moment was critical. An insurrection at Vienna had paralyzed the Austrian Government in its very capital. Lombardy and Venice were in open revolt, and Charles Albert, King of Sardinia, was moving with an army to their support. The Roman States and the Duchies were full of enthusiasm for the liberation of Italy from the Austrian power.

Pius IX. wished to see the peninsula free, but he was opposed to war and sought to form a national league of the different Italian States, which by negotiation should effect the desired result.

Naples, Tuscany, and some other States, were ready to join him; but Sardinia, full of projects for securing in its own hands the control of the whole peninsula, refused to send delegates to Rome. The war began. On the 24th of March, the Pope, checking the outbursts of the populace, sent an army under General Durando to protect his frontiers. His instructions were precise: "Know that you are marching solely to protect the frontiers of our States. Beware of crossing them, for by so doing, you will transgress my orders and place the pontifical troops in the attitude of aggressors, an attitude which can in no event be proper." General Durando, on reaching the frontier, pledged the Pope to a crusade of extermination against the Austrians, as enemies of the Cross of Christ; but the Pope promptly disavowed his course.

The war was brief and disastrous. Durando repulsed the Austrians, who attacked him at Vicenza; but Charles Albert was totally defeated before Milan by the Austrians, who exhibited unwonted energy and signal military skill. Then the pontifical army capitulated at Vicenza. The power of Austria seemed stronger than ever. This produced the greatest ferment at Rome. The revolutionary party became wildly violent. The city was completely in their hands. The cardinals were actually prisoners and the power of the Pope was defied. A savage mob called for the massacre of all priests, and was with difficulty restrained by Mamiani and other leaders who did not wish to shock the whole of Europe, and perhaps cause a foreign intervention which would have defeated all their plans.

The Pope in vain endeavored to counsel moderation. Italy was in a flame of excitement, and the revolution sought to destroy the influence of the Pope, as Head of the Church, by representing him in

Rome as the friend of Austria, and in Germany as the bitter opponent of everything German. At Rome, affairs were hourly more critical. The leaders of the populace demanded a change of ministry, the dismissal of Cardinal Antonelli, and the reorganization of the heads of the government by the appointment of laymen only. They insisted on the expulsion of the Austrian Ambassador, and an immediate declaration of war. The ministry had really resigned, but resumed their portfolios, to stand or fall with Cardinal Antonelli.

Pius IX. was now really a prisoner in his palace, which was surrounded by soldiers under the command of revolutionists. They were ordered to prevent the flight of the Pope. But Pius IX. did not yet despair of restoring peace to his States and calming the excited public feelings. He proposed Cardinal Altieri as prime minister, but Mamiani finally refusing to hold a portfolio under him, the difficult and dangerous position was assigned to Cardinal Ciacchi. On the 4th of May, the new ministry, with Count Mamiani as minister of the interior; Count Marchetti, minister of secular foreign affairs; Consultor Pascal de Rossi, minister of justice; Lunate, minister of finance; Prince Pamphili, of war, and the Duke of Rignano, minister of commerce, entered on its duties.

It was at once evident that the popular leaders thus forced on the Pope were acting in bad faith. With pretended liberality they proposed as member of the Council the Jesuit Father Vico, whom they had actually banished from Rome, where his wonderful astronomical researches had made him famous.

But the great effort of the ministry was to force the Pope to declare war on Austria. To this Pius IX. would not yield. He declared explicitly, " that he was aware that they sought to use him as an instrument to effect the designs of the agitators of Italy, who would no sooner attain their end than they would set him aside; that the project of depriving the sovereign Pontiff of his temporal domain had long been entertained; if they dared to wrest it from him, he would make his formal and solemn protest to the world."

Pius IX. had carried out the suggestions of the famous memorandum; and conclusively proved that the points urged in it were mischievous in their tendencies, not only to the peace of Rome, but of Europe. He could in all justice call upon the powers to remedy evils which they themselves had caused.

"He insisted that the right of declaring war is a special prerogative of sovereignty, and that he intended to yield it to none, and that consequently the address presented to him amounted really to a demand for his abdication, to which he would never consent."

The Parliament opened with the lay ministers hostile, and the House of Deputies full of revolutionists, the faithful people having generally abstained from voting, here as elsewhere the apathy of good citizens leaving the power for evil in the hands of the desperate and unprincipled. The address of Pius IX. inculcated the necessity of his keeping aloof from the struggle then going on.

But while Mamiani threw himself boldly into direct opposition with his sovereign, demanding his abdication and war with Austria, the inexorable logic of events was deciding the question.

The Austrians met the Italians with military skill and courage equal to their own. They defeated the Italians at Vicenza, and occupied Ferrara. On this the revolutionists who had derided all ecclesiastical intervention demanded the Pope's excommunication of the Austrians. The ministry resigned and a reign of terror began in Rome.

The crushing defeat of Charles Albert, at Custozza, left the Italian revolutionists hopeless. With Sardinia humbled to the dust, and the gallant king self-exiled, all thought of Rome's declaring war vanished. A new ministry, under Count Fabri, as representing the lay element, was formed. The Austrians, fully conceiving the position of the Pope in the recent events, at his request withdrew their forces from his territory. A word from the sovereign Pontiff effected what Italian arms had failed to accomplish.

The Parliament was prorogued to November, and the revolutionists prepared new schemes.

Amid all this turbulence which convulsed Rome, the Pope directed the affairs of the Church as though naught but the spiritual concerns absorbed his attention. In his remarkable pontificate we shall meet many occasions where amid peril or exile Pius IX. was planning or carrying out great designs for the good of the Church.

The state of the Church in Russia had been one of heroic suffering on the part of the faithful, and of terrible cruelties on the part of the imperial authorities.

Pius IX., in order to restore peace to the afflicted Church in Russia, had appointed Cardinal Lambruschini and the prelate John Carboli Bussi to meet Counts Bloudoff and Boutenieff, the envoys of the Czar, and arrange a treaty which would permit the sovereign Pontiff to bring the Catholic religion in the vast empire to a better condition, and provide more easily for the salvation of souls.

The results were most consoling. In the secret consistory of July 3, 1848, Pius IX. was able to announce to the cardinals that now it would be possible to appoint bishops of the Latin rite to sees which had long been vacant, both in Russia and in Poland. A new Episcopal see was to be erected at Kherson, with its chapter of canons and diocesan seminary, and a suffragan at Saratow. The Pope zealously endeavored to secure by the treaty the perfect freedom of the Catholic bishops in the administration of their dioceses. Provision was also made for the Catholics of the Armenian, Ruthenian, and other rites, who might be in the dioceses of bishops of the Latin rite, and with no bishop of their own. He did not indeed succeed in securing for the Catholics of Russia the desired freedom of communication with the Holy See which he desired, but still immense good was accomplished; property was restored to the Church, an intrusive lay officer no longer acted as a spy on meetings of the bishops, marriages were no longer subjected to the State Church. These concessions were made, however, only for the

Catholics of the Latin rite. The Ruthenians were still exposed to the penal laws. The sovereign Pontiff exhorted these persecuted Catholics to remain faithful and immovable in the unity of the Catholic Church, or to return to it promptly if they had fallen away in the hour of trial. The nominations of the bishops were to be made after consultation between the Czar and the Pope.

. On the 27th of August, Pius IX. visited the church of Saint Pantaleon to offer the holy sacrifice on the bi-centennial of the birth of St. Joseph Calasanctius. He there published a decree for the beatification of the venerable Peter Claver, a Jesuit priest, who devoted his whole life to the conversion and consolation of negro slaves in South America.

The court of Rome, about the same time, received the first diplomatic representative from the United States, who, on presenting his credentials, expressed the lively satisfaction felt in the United States at the noble efforts of Pius IX. to ameliorate the condition of his people. Pius IX. was also consoled to receive an envoy from the Queen of Spain, who had at last succeeded in restoring communication with the Holy See, and was endeavoring to revive religion in that once devotedly Catholic country.

In the storm of revolution which swept over Europe and agitated Italy to its depths, the Church was exposed to repeated attacks. In France, the noble archbishop of Paris, Mgr. Affre, died at the barricades while endeavoring to arrest the effusion of blood; and his heroic death gave the Church new honor even in the eyes of its opponents. In Germany, the government, anxious to see a national schism in the Catholic body, encouraged Ronge's attempt to found an independent German Catholic Church. In Switzerland, the government showed constant jealousy.

Amid all the perils of his position, Pius IX. watched with the eye of a vigilant father over all these exposed portions of his flock, consoling and encouraging the persecuted amid their struggles by words of apostolic fervor. On the 11th of September, he addressed the Sacred College on the virtues and merits of the illustrious archbishop of Paris, and urged on all the duty of praying that God would still the terrible tempest sweeping over the world and threatening, were it possible, to destroy the Church, and really causing the destruction of countless souls.

CHAPTER V.

The Ministry of Count Rossi.—A United Italy.—Assassination of Rossi.—The Quirinal besieged.—Pius IX. deserted by all but the Diplomatic Corps.—His Escape to Gaeta.—His Reception by the King of Naples.

The ministry of Mamiani, forced on the

Pope, had sought the good neither of the people nor of the Sovereign. It had been ruinously extravagant and productive of naught but evils. In all departments of the public service anarchy was fast replacing the former system and order. In this crisis Pius IX. called to the ministry a man of experience who had, as ambassador from France, been able to understand thoroughly the position of affairs. On the 16th of September, 1848, Count Pellegrino Rossi became Prime Minister, acting also as Minister of the Interior and of Finance. Cardinal Soglia was Secretary of State, but most of the other members were laymen.

It was a ministry that might have effected great good, but as it sought to render the people happy and prosperous under the rule of the Sovereign Pontiffs, it directly opposed the schemes of the revolutionists, and they resolved to overthrow it even by assassination.

Rossi, who possessed great executive ability, introduced economy and reform in place of Mamiani's disorder and extravagance; and while thus establishing a good government at home, he negotiated with the Kings of Naples and Sardinia and the Grand Duke of Tuscany a defensive confederation of the Italian States. This was the idea of Pius IX., under which each State retained its complete independence, but all were united to repel foreign aggression or intestine revolt. Sardinia met this proposal with duplicity. She could not altogether reject it, but already aimed through the revolution to acquire the sway of the whole peninsula.

The league would have defeated the revolution and liberated Italy. The secret societies in Rome, Turin, and Florence resolved that Rossi should be removed. Men were appointed to assassinate him, and on the 14th of November these by lot selected one of the number, Sante

Constantini, to strike the blow. He practiced on a dead body. The next day Count Rossi was warned, and Pius IX. urged him to take precautions for his safety. His associate ministers declined to allow the palace where the chambers met to be guarded by the carbineers. He saw that his doom was sealed, and doubtless felt that with so many enemies around pledged to his death, escape was impossible. When he heard that he was to be struck down as he entered the palace where the chambers sat, he replied, "I defend the cause of the Pope, and the cause of the Pope is the cause of God; I must and will go."

When his carriage drove into the court he saw that only members of the civic guard were on duty. He stepped from his carriage amid cries of: "Down with Rossi! death to Rossi! kill him!" A crowd at once gathered around and forced him aside from Righetto, one of the ministry who accompanied him. As he reached the building he was struck with a cane; he turned, and at that instant Constantini drove a dagger into his throat, severing the carotid artery. He reeled against the wall, made a few steps, and fell. "His murderer was not arrested," wrote the French minister to his government, "nor was any attempt made to seize him. Some gendarmes and civic guards were on the spot, but they did not interfere. The populace remained mute and cold. It was with difficulty that the minister's attendant could find any one to help him convey his master's body to an adjacent room. The Assembly, on whose very threshold the murder was committed, continued to read its minutes without interruption, and during the whole session no allusion was made to the event."

"Count Rossi died a martyr," said the great Pope, whom in the interests of the Roman people he sought to serve. "God will receive his soul in peace," and on the monument which he erected to his memory in the church of San Lorenzo were inscribed the words, "I undertook to protect the holiest of causes. God will have pity."

Such are secret societies. A true patriot, whose only aims were his country's, God's, and truth's, is marked out for death by a few nameless leaders, and men thought it a duty to execute their fearful orders. How can sensible men enter societies and bind themselves to violate the laws of God and man, to obey they know not whom, they know not why?

The murderer of Count Rossi was the hero of the mob, who the next day besieged the Quirinal. The army and civic guard sided with the rioters, making no effort to check them. For a time the Swiss Guard held the mere mob at bay, but says d'Harcourt, the French minister, who with the rest of the diplomatic corps stood beside the deserted Pontiff, "The mob were beginning to disperse, when, to our surprise, we beheld an unexpected spectacle. The civic guard, the gendarmerie, the line, and the Roman legion, to the number of some thousands in uniform, with music and drums, came and drew up in order of battle on the piazza of the Quirinal, and joined by such of the mob as remained, opened fire on the windows of the Quirinal palace. Some of the balls penetrated the apartments, and one killed a prelate (Mgr. Palma) who was in his chamber. As the Swiss continued to display a bold attitude, and it was thought that a determined resistance would be offered, cannon were brought to batter down the doors of the Pope's palace."

The Pope evinced the greatest coolness and firmness, but as it was impossible to hold out, negotiations were entered into. A committee entered to present to Cardinal Soglia a programme of their demands. The Pope's only reply was that he would consider it. Then a deputation of officers of carbineers was sent in. Pius IX. received them in person, surrounded by the ambassadors of France, Spain, Bavaria, Portugal, and Russia. The Pope, to their demand, replied that they in fact asked him to abdicate, and that he had no power to do. Roused at the insult thus offered to the sovereign Pontiff by poltroon officers of his own army overawed by a mob and its hidden leaders, Martinez de la Rosa exclaimed, " Go, gentlemen ; tell the leaders of this revolt that if they persist in their odious project they must march over my dead body to reach the sacred person of the sovereign Pontiff. But tell them that the vengeance of Spain will be terrible."

The Pope was now a prisoner in the palace. A provisional government was formed with Sterbini at the head, and Charles, prince of Canino, who had led the students of the Sapienza in the attack on the palace. They sought to force a new ministry on the Pope, but he said: "I am here a prisoner. They have wished to deprive me of my guard and put me in the hands of others. My course at this moment, when I am deprived of all support and all material power, can have but one object, to avoid, at any cost, the useless shedding of a single drop of fraternal blood in my behalf. To this fear I yield, but at the same time, I wish you and all Europe to know that I do not even nominally take any part in the government, and that I remain absolutely a stranger to its acts. I have forbidden any abuse of my name, I have even forbidden the use of the ordinary formulas."

Sterbini and Bonaparte attempted to disband the Swiss Guard: they yielded only at the command of Pius IX.

The sovereign Pontiff saw himself now alike unable to govern the Church or his

States while remaining in Rome. A secret flight was the only course open to him.

"One consideration more than another," says Maguire,* "was powerful with the Pope—that the direction of those affairs which related to the Church was not only interfered with, but was rendered wholly impossible. At first, he was doubtful as to the course which he should take, or the resolution to which he should come; and in this state of suspense he remained for two or three days, when he received a letter from France, from the bishop of Valence. In this letter the bishop acquainted his Holiness that a little silver case having come into his possession, which had served Pius VII., of blessed memory, to keep therein a consecrated particle, in order that he might have the most Holy Sacrament as a solace during the sad exile to which tyranny and infidelity had con-

---

* "Rome and its Ruler," p. 89.

demned him, he was happy to have it conveyed to Pope Pius IX. as a memorial of one of his holy predecessors, and as an object perhaps not useless during the events that were taking place in those days. On the receipt of this precious memorial, the Pope no longer delayed, or hesitated as to the course which he should take; and he accordingly resolved upon abandoning Rome. At first, he deliberated upon what place to select for his stay, but as the Spanish court had offered him their hospitality, and as the ambassador, Signor Martinez de la Rosa, assured him of the immediate arrival of a steamer belonging to that nation in the harbor of Civita Vecchia, the Pope thought that this would be an opportune means whereby to effect his escape; but the Spanish steamer being retarded from day to day, and the state of affairs in Rome becoming more and more alarming, the Pope intimated to the Spanish ambassador that he purposed setting out at once, and that orders might be given to the captain of the steamer, when he should arrive at Civita Vecchia, to sail to the port of Gaeta, whither he had determined to proceed. The intended flight had been already communicated to upward of fifty persons, ecclesiastics and seculars, and everything was in readiness for its accomplishment. It took place in the following manner. The Duke d'Harcourt, minister of France, on the evening of the 24th, drove up, with couriers and torches, to the usual entrance. Leaving his carriage at the foot of the stairs by which all who seek an audience with the Holy Father ascend, he was introduced as though for a solemn reception. Proceeding at once to the apartments of the Pope, he aided him to exchange his white soutane for the black cassock of an ordinary priest, gave him a pair of large spectacles and a cloak. When his Holiness was ready, the duke began to read in a loud voice, as if submitting some important document to the immediate decision of the Pope, and thus deceived the guards without. Meanwhile Pius IX., guided by his attendant, the Cavalier Filippani, passed through a series of apartments, guided only by a taper, which was suddenly extinguished by a draft, compelling Filippani to return, to the great dismay of the duke. But Providence guided them. The revolutionists watched in front only; they reached the cortile of the Quirinal by the Swiss door unperceived, but were nearly betrayed, as they entered the carriage waiting there, by a good domestic, who recognizing the Pope fell on his knees, but rose at a warning gesture, unperceived by the civic guard who were exchanging greetings with Filippani.

The carriage, with its precious but unsuspected passenger, drove rapidly amid the soldiers in the Piazza and through one street after another, crossing the Corso and passing beneath the shadow of the Coliseum, till it reached the monastery of St. Marcellino e Pietro, where Count Spaur, the Bavarian minister, awaited him. Thence the illustrious fugitive drove rapidly to the Albano gate, to meet the post-chaise which had been prepared for his journey to Gaeta.

Here the faithful Filippani left Pius IX., placing in his hands a package of secret papers, the seals, a breviary, and a few clothes, the whole traveling outfit of the sovereign Pontiff. He closed the door with a good-bye to the supposed Abate, Count Spaur mounted the box, and the fresh horses started for the St. John gate. Hailed there by the sentry, "Who goes there?" the reply, "The Ambassador of Bavaria and Doctor Aletz," sufficed to obtain the word to pass. The Countess Spaur awaited them in another conveyance, in the valley of Ariccia. As the

Pope drove up, five carbineers, on patrol, approached. "Is that you, doctor," said the Countess, "you have kept us waiting." Unsuspectingly the carbineers aided his Holiness to enter the Countess' carriage. He sat behind with the Countess, her son Maximilian, and his tutor, Liebl, in front. The Count again occupied the box with the driver.

The carriage drove rapidly on. The Pope, in silent prayer, pressing to his heart the pyx of Pius VII., containing the Blessed Sacrament; the rest full of awe at their proximity to the Father of the Faithful, and full of anxiety for the result. As though penetrating their secret thought, the Pope first broke silence, saying, "Be calm, God is with us. I carry the Blessed Sacrament on my person." He continued in silent prayer or reciting the breviary with Father Liebl.

At Forli, while changing horses, one of the postillions remarked, "How much that doctor looks like a picture of the Pope I have at home," but turned at once to talk of something else, and all breathed more freely.

On leaving Terracina he asked the Countess to tell him the moment they reached the Neapolitan frontier. All again was silent, till at last she cried, "Holy Father, we are there!" Then he burst into tears and thanked God for his protection, reciting the Te Deum in thanksgiving.

It was just before daybreak. Relieved from a terrible anxiety, they drove on, and at half-past nine reached the mole of Gaeta, where Cardinal Antonelli and the first secretary of the Spanish legation awaited them. Count Spaur at once left them for Naples, bearing a letter from the Pope to the King of Naples, written at the Villa Cicerone, announcing that he had come to solicit shelter at his hands, but that he did not wish by his presence to cause any complications during the stay he was compelled to make while awaiting a vessel to bear him to Spain.

The Duke d'Harcourt, after keeping up his reading as long as he deemed necessary to enable the Pope to pass beyond the limits of the city, came out of the apartments of his Holiness, and giving the sentinels to understand that the Pope had retired, drove off, and at once prepared to follow him to Gaeta.

At that city the Pope proceeded to the bishop's palace, but that prelate was absent, and the household were too suspicious of the strangers to open the apartments to them. He returned to Gaeta, and the party were summoned before the commandant of the fortress, to which Cardinal Antonelli at once repaired, but failed to disarm his suspicions as to the mysterious party at the inn.

Count Spaur had meanwhile driven in all haste to Naples, where he at once proceeded to the Pope's Nuncio. He could scarcely induce that prelate to believe his words and present him to the king. They drove to the palace, and reaching it at midnight, delivered to Ferdinand the letter of Pius IX. He read it with wonder, and heard in tears the account of his escape. Then he ran to the apartments of the queen and his children, crying, "Arise! the Pope is at Gaeta; we must start to-night to throw ourselves at his feet, and offer him our respectful homage."

Two steamers, the *Tancred* and the *Robert*, were at once got ready; the king ordered a number of articles for the Pope's immediate use, clothing, furniture, plate, and at six o'clock he embarked on the *Tancred* with the queen and his whole family, the Bavarian minister, and a numerous suite.

The steamers appeared off Gaeta almost simultaneously with a French frigate bear-

GAETA, THE RESIDENCE OF PIUS IX. WHEN DRIVEN FROM ROME.

ing the Duke d'Harcourt. In a short time all met at the governor's palace, and the mystery was solved.

Ferdinand II., could not restrain his tears on beholding the Head of the Church appear, bereft of all the attributes of his exalted dignity, almost alone, leaning on a cane, but gentle, calm, as benignant under his black hat as under the triple crown. The queen knelt on the staircase with her children, the whole court imitated her example, nor did they rise till they received the blessing of the illustrious guest whom heaven had sent.

The king at once used every argument to induce the Pope to-accept his hospitality and remain at Gaeta, a safe and tranquil spot, near the Roman frontier, amid a faithful people and protected by a formidable fortress. He gave him his own palace, and took up his residence in a house at a short distance, and showed every courtesy and care toward the cardinals and other personages, who gradually formed a little court around the Pope.

The Spanish minister had on the part of the queen offered Pius IX. a home in her kingdom; but the devotion of Ferdinand II. prevailed, and with the approval of all the powers, Gaeta became, for a time, the residence of the august exile.

Not far from Gaeta there is a celebrated sanctuary of the Holy Trinity; the Sovereign Pontiff expressing a wish to offer his devotions there, set out with the king and queen, the princes, cardinals, and the diplomatic corps. On the way the Pope alighted, and from a rising ground bestowed his benediction on the king and the troops who surrounded him. At the grotto of the sanctuary the superior of the religious community intrusted with its care celebrated the holy sacrifice in the presence of the supreme Pontiff. At the close of the mass Pius IX. approached the altar, and while all were expecting to behold him turn and bless them, Pius IX. knelt and pronounced aloud this fervent prayer, which moved all to tears:

"Eternal God, my august Father and Lord, behold at thy feet thy unworthy vicar, who entreats thee with his whole heart to pour out upon him from thy eternal throne thy divine benediction. O my God, direct his steps, sanctify his intentions, guide his mind, govern his actions. May he be here, where thou hast led him in thy admirable Providence, or in any other portion of thy fold to which he may go, a worthy instrument of thy glory, and that of thy Church, which, alas! is assailed by thy enemies. If, to appease thy wrath so justly enkindled by the many indignities that are offered to thee, in word, in action, and by the abuse of the press, his own life may be an agreeable holocaust to thy Divine Heart, he consecrates it to thee from this moment. Thou hast given it to him, to thee only belongs the right of taking it away when it may please thee; but, O my God, let thy glory triumph, let thy Church be victorious. Preserve the good, support the feeble, and may the arm of thy omnipotence arouse all who are slumbering in darkness, and in the shadow of death. Bless, O Lord, the ruler who is here prostrate before thee; bless his consort and his family; bless all his subjects, and his faithful and honored soldiery; bless the cardinals, the bishops, and all the clergy, that they may accomplish in the peaceful ways of thy law, the sanctification of the people. Then may we hope, not only to be delivered during our mortal pilgrimage from the snares of the impious and the machinations of wicked men, but to reach that place which affords eternal safety: *ut hic et in æternum, te auxiliante, salvi et liberi esse mereamur.*"

CHAPTER VI.

Pius IX. at Gaeta.—His Protest.—Rome in the hands of the Revolution.—Intervention of the Catholic Powers.—General Oudinot Recovers Rome. — Napoleon's Tortuous Policy.—Pius IX. Invited to America.—Encyclical on the Immaculate Conception.—His Work at Gaeta.

From Gaeta Pius IX. addressed to his subjects and to the Catholic world this protest:

"Pius IX. to the Roman people:

"The outrage committed within the last days against our person, and the openly-avowed intention of continuing these acts of violence (which the Almighty, inspiring men's minds with sentiments of union and moderation, has prevented), have compelled us to separate ourselves temporarily from our subjects and children, whom we love and ever shall love. The reasons which have induced us to take this important step—heaven knows how painful it is to our hearts—have arisen from the necessity of our enjoying free liberty in the exercise of the sacred duties of the Holy See, as, under the circumstances by which we were then affected, the Catholic world might reasonably doubt of the freedom of that exercise. The acts of violence of which we complain can alone be attributed to the machinations which have been used, and the measures that have been taken by a class of men degraded in the face of Europe and the world. This is the more evident, as the wrath of the Almighty has already fallen on their souls, and as it will call down on them, sooner or later, the punishment which is prescribed for them by his Church.

"We recognize humbly, in the ingratitude of these misguided children, the anger of the Almighty, who permits their misfortunes as an atonement for the sins of ourselves and those of our people. But still we cannot, without betraying the sacred duties imposed on us, refrain from protesting formally against their acts, as we did do verbally on the 16th of November, of painful memory, in presence of the whole Diplomatic Corps, who on that occasion honorably encircled us, and brought comfort and consolation to our souls, in recognizing that a violent and unprecedented sacrilege had been committed. That protest we did intend, as we now do, openly and publicly to repeat, inasmuch as we yielded only to violence, and because we were and are desirous it should be made known that all proceedings emanating from such acts of violence were and are devoid of all efficacy and legality. This protest is as a necessary consequence of the malicious labor of these wicked men, and we publish it from the suggestion of our conscience, stimulated as it has been by the circumstances in which we were placed, and the impediments offered to the exercises of our sacred duties. Nevertheless, we confide upon the Most High that the continuance of these evils may be abridged, and we humbly supplicate the God of heaven to avert his wrath, in the language of the prophet—'*Memento, Domine, David, et omnis mansuetudinis ejus?*' In order that the city of Rome and our States be not deprived of a legal executive, we have nominated a governing commission, composed of the following persons: 'The Cardinal Castracane, President, Monsignor Roberto Roberti, Prince Roviano, Prince Barberini, Marquis Bevilacqua di Bologna, Lieutenant-General Zucchi.'

"In confiding to the said governing commission the temporary direction of public affairs, we recommend to our subjects and children, without exception, the conservation of tranquillity and good order. Finally, we desire and commend that daily and earnest prayers shall be offered for the safety of our person and that the peace of the world may be preserved, especially that of our State of Rome, where and with whose children, our heart shall be wherever we in person may dwell within the fold of Christ. And in fulfillment of our duty as supreme Pontiff, we thus humbly and devoutly invoke the Great Mother of Mercy, and the holy apostles, Peter and Paul, for their intercession that the city and State of Rome may be saved from the wrath of the Omnipotent God.

"Pius Papa IX.
"Gaeta, November 28."

In Rome the escape of the Pope from their hands disconcerted entirely the plans of the revolutionists. Pius IX. at Gaeta, was recognized by all the great powers as still the sovereign of Rome, the ruler of the patrimony of St. Peter. The ministers of France, Spain, and Bavaria had taken part in his departure from Rome. It was unexampled that a sovereign in exile should be so regarded universally, yet the Pope was recognized not by Catholic powers only, but by England, Prussia, and Russia. This made it impossible for the revolutionists to obtain recognition; conscious of this they sent a deputation to Gaeta to induce the Pope to return to Rome, but he declined to receive them. "He could not treat," said Cardinal Antonelli, in his reply, "with a defunct ministry and a Parliament which he had dissolved." Then they threw off the mask, and on the 12th of December, established a Junta, overthrowing the Parliament, but on the 29th these called a National Assembly of the Roman States.

The enemies of the Church at Rome and elsewhere exulted at the overthrow of the Papacy; but never did men delude themselves more grossly with their own desires. A sovereign Pontiff reigning in peace at Rome, as many of his predecessors had done, is scarcely known in person to the millions of Catholics scattered throughout the world. He is the Pope, revered and honored, but scarcely known except in name. Bishops and occasionally priests would go from time to time to Rome, and on their return a temporary interest be excited in the reigning sovereign Pontiff. During the last century the reverse has been the case. The sufferings of Pius VI., Pius VII., and of Pius IX., endeared them personally to all Catholic hearts. Every Catholic child knows that Pius IX. is the reigning Pope, and, from the constant reproductions of his portrait, is familiar with that benign and saintly face. From the time of his exile to Gaeta, Pius IX. has been known and loved by his flock as no Pope had ever been before.

On the 1st of January, the Pope again addressed the people of his States, warning them against the pretended National Assembly convoked by the wretches then in power at Rome. Regardless of his protests the leaders of the revolution established a Supreme Provisional Junta of State; but against this Pius IX. protested in a document issued January 17, 1849.

On the 8th of February, the Assembly under the guidance of Mazzini, who had arrived in Rome, declared the Pope, in fact and of right, deprived of the temporal government of the Roman States; but at the same time declared that he should have every guarantee of independence necessary for the exercise of his spiritual powers.

The world, however, considered that if a Roman mob had the power to authorize the Pope to exercise his spiritual functions, it must have the power to forbid; and no sensible person could concede that they had either.

France made the first move. The faithful revived the Peter's Pence, which in the ages of faith had been such a resource to the sovereign Pontiffs. The new-formed Republic, on the 27th of November, dispatched a fervent Catholic, M. de Corcelles, with a brigade of 3,500 men to intervene in the name of the French Republic, and restore to his Holiness his personal liberty, if he was deprived of it. This did not satisfy the heart of France. In the session of the 30th, Count Montalembert nobly said: "The person of the Pope is infinitely dear to us and infinitely sacred; but there is something dearer and more sacred in our eyes, it is his authority."

General Cavaignac addressed the Pope, offering him the hospitality of France. Prince Napoleon, aiming at his uncle's throne, and reading more clearly the Catholic heart of the people, wrote to the Nuncio in France, to disclaim all knowledge or approval of the conduct of the Prince of Canino, his cousin, and deploring that that member of the Bonaparte family had not seen that the maintenance of the temporal sovereignty of the venerable Head of the Church was intimately connected with the luster of Catholicity as well as with the liberty and independence of Italy. Napoleon rose to the throne of France by giving the support of his country to the Pope; the scepter slipped from his grasp when he withdrew it.

Spain first declared for an armed intervention. In a diplomatic note of December 21, 1848, she declared, "The question is no longer whether the Pope's liberty shall be protected, but whether his authority shall be restored in a firm and stable manner and assured against all violence. The Pontifical sovereignty is of such importance for Christian States that it can by no means be left at the mercy of a small part of the Catholic world like the Roman States."

On the 18th of April, 1849, Cardinal Antonelli, in the name of Pius IX., for-

CARDINAL JAMES ANTONELLI.

mally solicited the aid of France, Austria, Spain, and other Catholic nations. All responded to the appeal except Sardinia, and the plenipotentiaries met at Gaeta.

In this conference it was agreed that Austria should occupy Romagna, and the king of Naples the southern part of the States of the Church. Spain offered to reduce Rome, the only difficult and dangerous part of the plan; but France claimed it of right as the Eldest Daughter of the Church. The decision was immediately acted upon. The Austrians, after defeating at Novara the king of Sardinia, who was really supporting the radicals, occupied the Legations with fifty thousand men, taking Bologna and Ancona in May and June. Five thousand Spanish troops landed near Terracina, on the 29th of April, and reduced that city. On the 1st of May, twelve hundred Neapolitans entered Velletri.

A French army under General Oudinot,

Duke of Reggio, landed without opposition at Civita Vecchia, on the 25th of April, and marched on Rome.

The condition of that city, after the departure of the Holy Father, had been terrible indeed. A mob of criminals of every description from all parts of Italy had gathered there, and were the real masters of Rome. When, on the 9th of February, the Assembly, which made it almost a rule that every member should have been in prison or in the galleys, declared the rule of the Pope abolished, the peaceful, quiet citizens were struck dumb. They had stood idly by, till the Pope in the hands of the revolutionists was powerless. Now they beheld what masters had succeeded the mild and gentle rule of the Popes.

Yet there were shouts and acclamations. The clubs collected their followers, and by wild declamation gathered many of the young and excitable around them.

A triumvirate, consisting of Armellini, Montecchi, and Salicetti, ruled for six weeks; then the two latter gave place to Saffi and Mazzini. Pius IX., the venerable representative of order and truth, had been replaced by Mazzini, the chief of the enemies of Christ, the very incarnation of anarchy and social dissolution.

The representatives of all the foreign powers had followed the Pope to Gaeta. Nearly all the cardinals, with many prelates and ecclesiastics, had imitated their example. Foreign residents, not daring to face the scenes that might be enacted, withdrew. The wealthy retired to their country seats, the higher institutions of learning were closed, commerce and business were suspended. Rome, drained of its best and worthiest citizens, was filled with thieves, vagabonds, and assassins. A reign of terror exceeding in horror that of revolutionary France ensued.

At first they pretended a respect for

religion. The new Government heard high mass in St. Peter's on Easter Day, after finding a fallen priest base enough to say mass and give a benediction in mockery of the sovereign Pontiff. They decreed the restoration and repairs of all the churches; but in a few days proceeded to confiscate them all, abolish religious orders, seize on the sacred vessels, leaving only a single chalice to each church; they even melted down the bells to make cannon. Churches became ballrooms, theaters, or baths; the Vatican and Quirinal were converted into hospitals; convents were so many barracks. Soon every church showed that the reign of Antichrist had begun. The walls were polluted, the paintings torn down, statues of the saints mutilated, their reliquaries rifled; even the Catacombs were profaned and the bones of animals piled in among the bones of the martyrs of the primitive Church. The Blessed Sacrament was exposed to insults and profanations that are horrible even to think of.

A few months made the city look as though it had been swept by a horde of barbarians, and a quarter of a century has not effaced the destruction of that revolutionary rule of 1849.

Murder was unpunished and tolerated. No one dared walk the street in the dress of a priest, except at the peril of his life. These assassinations or executions as they were called amounted in a few weeks to one thousand. A Custom House officer named Zambianchi at the head of a band of assassins imprisoned and slew at his pleasure; fourteen priests died at his hands in one day. The bodies of these victims were afterwards found in a common grave in the garden of the Benedictines near the Janiculum. The Triumvirate looked on, till the general movement of the Catholic powers cautioned some moderation. Then a number of priests were rescued from his bloody hands.

The Pope might justly invoke the powers to save his people from such monsters!

General Oudinot moved on Rome, and disaffection to the usurpers began to appear even in the civic guards, who had been so unfaithful to Pius IX., but now saw their misguided folly. Mazzini disarmed several battalions. Had the French general pushed on, the city would have fallen without a blow. But Napoleon, Prince President of France, had yielded reluctantly to the movement. He wished still to avoid any positive action against the Italian revolutionists. Oudinot was hampered by orders, and by the presence of de Lesseps, who was sent to treat with the Triumvirs. This gave time for Garibaldi with a band of desperate adventurers to enter Rome. A spirit of resistance was at once aroused, and Garibaldi organized the defense with energy and cunning.

When Oudinot, misled by crafty announcements from Rome that the French had only to march in, appeared with four thousand men before the Cavallegieri Gate of the city, he was received with such a well-directed fire of musketry and artillery that he had to withdraw his troops, leaving as prisoners some who had been allowed to enter another gate.

France was more loyal to the Holy Father than the ambitious President, and compelled him to give Oudinot forces sufficient to reduce Rome.

On the 1st of June, the French troops stormed the Pamphili and Orsini villas on Mount Janiculum, though obstinately defended by volunteers from Lombardy. Garibaldi, with the best and most reckless of his soldiers, held the church of St. Pancras. This too was carried after a fearful carnage.

Pius IX. had asked that Rome should not be bombarded. The cannon of the French were opened only on the walls. On the 29th of June, when the Catholic world was celebrating the feast of the Prince of the Apostles, the walls were breached, and the storming parties of the liberating army dashed into the city and held their ground. The Triumvirs asked a suspension of arms. Mazzini fled from the people whom he had outraged and oppressed in the name of liberty. Garibaldi retreated with the shattered remnant of his force toward the Adriatic. Barricades remained, but the courage of the desperate revolutionists who still attempted to hold out soon failed them. On the 3d of July, General Oudinot entered Rome at the head of his army, and dispatching Colonel Niel to Pius IX. as bearer of the keys of the city, began the work of restoring order.

The remaining soldiers of the revolutionary forces were disarmed; their clubs and political rendezvous suppressed. Murder, violence, and robbery were checked by prompt and unsparing punishment. Gradually the citizens returned, the churches were again opened; schools resumed their usual courses, and Rome began to wear once more its usual appearance.

The Pope appointed as a Council of Regency, till his return, Cardinals Della Genga, Altieri, and Vannicelli. But the tortuous policy of Napoleon at once raised obstacles to the return of Pius IX. from his exile. In a letter to Edgar Ney, whom he sent as a sort of unofficial representative, he demanded from the Pope a general amnesty, the secularization of the government, the adoption of the Code Napoleon, and a liberal government. The Prince President sought to reimpose on the Pope the very points of the Memorandum of 1831 which Pius IX. had in the good faith of his heart sought to carry out, and which had borne such fatal fruits.

The professed anxiety for liberal institutions came strangely too from the lips of a man who was at that very moment plotting the overthrow of the French Republic and the restoration of the Empire.

For a time these intrigues deprived Rome of her Pontiff King.

He remained at Gaeta, recognized as Sovereign of the Papal States by the civilized world, and what was more, recognized by the Catholics in all lands as the Vicar of Christ, doubly endeared to them by suffering, exile, hatred, and persecution. From Gaeta he nominated bishops or confirmed the names submitted: he replied to consultations addressed to him concerning difficulties that arose, or granted spiritual powers and dispensations.

Pilgrims came from all parts of the

world, bearing to the feet of the saintly exile the expression of their veneration. He received them all. Addresses without number poured in from all lands. He replied to them all.

The course of events compelled the bishops in various countries to assemble, some for the first time in many years, and all submitted the result of their deliberations to the banished Pope. America, happier in her freedom, assembled under the Pontiff's direction, and in his name a Plenary Council of all the Catholic archbishops and bishops in the United States at Baltimore. Before its solemn opening, on hearing that Pope Pius IX. would probably visit France, the hierarchy of this new-risen Church through the Archbishop of Baltimore, invited him to extend his journey to America and preside at the Plenary Council. He replied as follows:

"Pius, PP. IX.

"Venerable brother, health and apostolical benediction:

"We have received with the greatest pleasure the expression of your particular regard and love for us, and, well aware of your religion and faith in the Church, we are not surprised to learn that the momentous trials which the head of the Church, the Roman Pontiff, has to contend with have filled you, venerable brother, with the most bitter grief. Although our afflictions would overpower us, without a special assistance from God, yet being able to do all things in him who strengtheneth us, we are prepared to suffer most cheerfully any kind of tribulation, if our labors will only contribute to the peace, advantage, and safety of the Church. And having the divine promise that Christ the Lord will be with his Church to the consummation of the world, and that the gates of hell will never prevail against it, we are exceedingly animated and encouraged by this belief, and amidst the most trying difficulties we experience a great consolation, while we wait for assistance from above.

"God, indeed, will not be wanting to his promises; commanding the winds and the sea, he will make peace, and will show, as you have well said, venerable brothers, that the present dreadful storm has been raised for manifesting the greater glory of his name, and achieving the more brilliant triumph of his holy Church. As you have signified your earnest wish that we should assist at the Provincial Council which you are about to hold, according to custom, with our other venerable brethren, the bishops of the United States of America, be assured that nothing could afford us more pleasure, nothing could be more grateful to our hearts than to enjoy the presence and conversation of yourself and the same venerable brethren, to embrace you all with affection, to express to you the sentiments of profound regard which we entertain for each one of you, and to congratulate you upon the pastoral zeal for which you are distinguished, and the well-known solicitude with which you labor so assiduously, in the discharge of your functions, to extend the glory of God, to promote our most holy religion, and to secure the salvation of the beloved flocks committed to your care.

"But as, in the existing times and circumstances, it would be impossible for us to comply with your invitation, as your wisdom will easily understand, venerable brother, we request you to make known to the prelates these sentiments of our mind, and to inform them of the apostolical benediction, which from our inmost heart we affectionately impart to you, to them, to all the clergy of that country, and to all your faithful people.

"Given at Gaeta, the 8th day of March,

1849, in the third year of our pontificate.

"Pius PP. IX."

From Gaeta, Pius IX., adopting a new method of ascertaining the opinions of the bishops throughout the universe, whom it was not possible under existing circumstances to assemble in a general council, consulted them on a point very dear to his heart, a decisive definition in regard to the Immaculate Conception of the Blessed Virgin. On the 2d of February, 1849, he heard some proceedings in the cause of the beatification of a venerable servant of God, Anthony Mary Zaccaria, and a decree was issued recognizing his heroic virtues; then, in reply to an address, he spoke at length of the troubles which afflicted the Church at large, and seemed to center on Rome:

"O Rome, Rome! God is my witness that I daily raise my voice to the Lord, and, prostrate as a suppliant, ardently beseech him to arrest the scourge which desolates thee, and daily presses with new weight upon thee! I implore him to stay the suggestions of the most perverse doctrines, and to banish from the walls and the whole State the political declaimers who abuse the name of the people."

That same day he addressed an encyclical letter to the patriarchs, primates, archbishops, and bishops of the world. After reciting the almost universal appeal of Christian piety in favor of this belief, so that the complete manifestation seemed sufficiently prepared by the liturgy, by the formal requests of the bishops, and by the labors of learned theologians, he proceeds to declare that this general disposition was in perfect unison with his own thoughts, and that amid the horrible calamities of the Church, he would be greatly consoled to add a new gem to the crown of the all-powerful Virgin, and to acquire a special claim on her protection.

With this view he had, as he now announced, established a commission of cardinals to examine the question, and he invited all his venerable brethren in the episcopate to transmit their opinions to him, and to blend their supplications with his to obtain light from on high.

The belief that Mary had, in the designs of the eternal Trinity, been exempted from the consequences of Adam's fall, to fit her for the exalted dignity to which she was to be raised as Mother of our Redeemer, had prevailed among the faithful in all ages, though not authoritatively taught. During the ages of faith, when all men believed in the fall of man, the doctrine of original sin, and the necessity for redemption of the grace purchased by the precious blood of Christ, subtle disputants in the schools had on the one side put the doctrine in a scholastic proposition, and on the other raised objections. But the faith of the pious was untouched, and when the discussions seemed likely to cool and diminish piety, the Popes had interposed and set bounds to the opposition.

Now that the fundamental doctrines of Christianity were everywhere openly denied; when Europe was actually in the hands of secret societies, which, ignoring or denying Christ, sought, as the first great step in their plans, the destruction of the Church, Pius IX. believed the moment come for a solemn definition that would give new life to Catholic piety and faith.

On the 20th of April, 1849, he addressed the cardinals in a secret consistory as he would have done at Rome; and his allocution reviewed the whole situation of the Church, and the evils that afflicted it, as well as the position in which he found himself, and the fearful condition of Rome and his States, where vice was rampant, religion proscribed, and the most profligate of either sex were now placed by authority at the bedside of the dying, instead of the ministers of religion.

This devotion of the Pope to his spiritual duties, these purely theological thoughts, when the very ground seemed crumbling beneath his feet, drew on the sovereign Pontiff the sarcasms of human wisdom. They did not at first perceive that this step of Pius IX., which many are too ignorant or blind to understand, was a triumphant answer to all the errors of the age. The very form of promulgation adopted drew all the churches of the world into closer union with Rome. Piety was aroused, and the doctrine, old as the Church, became a source of life and strength. Then impiety raged against the new dogma, which it finally saw to be a weapon it could not parry and a shield it could not pierce.

Never was the Pope more actively engaged in the affairs of the Church than at Gaeta. The turmoil of civil affairs compelled the bishops in France and Germany to assemble. The governments that had sought to fetter the Church were now glad to leave her at liberty. Councils were held and their deliberations came to Gaeta for the approval of the successor of St. Peter.

In Tuscany the bishops in the Chamber of Deputies protested against the irreligious press. The Pope wrote to sustain their zeal. Brilliant minds in Italy had been dazzled by the glare of liberal promises; three priests, whose influence with learned and unlearned was great, Gioberti, Rosmini, Ventura, broached errors which Pius IX. condemned; two submitted to the decision, renouncing all self-love; but Gioberti, in his self-will, preferred to forfeit his high prerogative of Catholic.

Under his impulse efforts were made everywhere to secure freedom of education for Catholics. On all sides every form of error opposed to Catholic truth bends its energies to secure the children of Catholics, and train them up in hatred, or shame, or ignorance of their faith. It is the great battle of the age; and Pope Pius IX. has constantly urged unwearied vigilance and earnestness in the struggle. We must train our children for heaven, or the world will train them for destruction. But the question of freedom of education is subtly involved, and so it was in France. Pius IX. counseled and encouraged the bishops in the struggle.

In Naples, Pius IX. obtained in May, 1848, freedom for the diocesan seminaries; the bishops were relieved from State interference in their direction. A concordat with Leopold, Grand Duke of Tuscany, obtained similar liberty. Francis Joseph, of Austria, abolished the odious proscriptions of Joseph II. against the Church and its liberties. By an imperial ordinance of April 18, 1850, he declared the faithful and the clergy free to correspond with the Pope—for our readers will hardly credit it, yet in fact for nearly a hundred years no Catholic bishop in that country could write to the Pope without submitting his letter and its reply to the government, and even Protestant officers thus decided on Catholic questions. By the just rules of Francis Joseph, bishops could now issue pastorals to their flock, pronounce ecclesiastical censures, suspend clergymen who violated the laws of the Church, and regulate their dioceses, without first asking the permission of government. Pius IX., in his allocution of May 20, 1850, gave due praise to the monarch who had thus delivered the Church from a cruel bondage.

But while his heart was consoled to see the Church thus left free to pursue her great work, he was grieved to find Sardinia joining the revolution in all its hostility to the Church and to the true interests of human society. The Siccardi law passed in that country abolished the concordat existing between the government and the Pope, confiscated the property and revenues of the Church, placed the pulpit under police supervision, and struck a blow at the sacrament of matrimony, by declaring marriage a mere civil contract. The noble archbishop of Turin, Monsignor Franzoni, for addressing his clergy on the rights of the Church, was torn from his palace and flung into a dungeon, consoled by his conscience and by the encouraging words of the Pope.

Amid all these cares of the universal Church, Pius IX. lived his simple life at Gaeta; visiting the churches and sanctuaries, taking his walks among the pious people, who looked with reverence on that benign countenance, and that head prematurely whitened by the hand of care. The cathedral of Gaeta became a new St. Peter's. The royal family came in the spring to reside near the Pope. They took part in the functions at the cathedral, where, during Holy Week, Pius IX. officiated as at Rome, and gave his blessing to kneeling thousands from the balcony of the bishop's palace.

On the 4th of September, Pius IX. sailed to Naples with the royal family, one member just baptized, and another confirmed by him. The next day he landed at the haven of Portici, at the spot where the first Pope had landed eighteen centuries before.

Here his life was a repetition of that at Gaeta; he went about blessing and consoling.

ROME.

CHAPTER VII.

Pius IX. Restored to Rome.—His Edict of September 12, 1849. — His Return to Rome.—The English Hierarchy.—The Church and the World.

The attitude of the President of the French Republic had brought affairs into a strange position. Rome was rescued from the revolutionists and in the hands of France; Austria held the legations; Naples and Spain other parts of the Papal States. France had attempted to dictate to the Pope the line of policy he was to pursue. Pius IX. could not sacrifice his independence. The French ministry, lacking alike noble courage to condemn Napoleon's schemes, or hardihood to approve them, was dismissed. The President abandoned his ideas for a time. The Pope was left free to rule the Papal States.

On the 12th of September, 1849, Pius

IX., by an edict issued at Portici, regulated the form of government for his States. A Council of State was established, which was to give advice on all proposed laws before they were submitted to the sovereign sanction, and on all questions of importance in the administration. There was to be a consulta for finances, a council in each province, while the existing municipal institutions were to be maintained. A general amnesty was proclaimed, from which were excluded only those who had taken part in the revolutionary government, or held office under it, and of all who, after profiting by the Pope's first amnesty, had in any way acted against the promise then given.

This edict was published in Rome on the 20th, by a Papal Commission of four cardinals, and the Pontifical Government again duly inaugurated. Rome began to breathe freely, and a feeling of security was once more felt as the people emerged from the recent terrible dream. The wealthy returned, strangers poured in, the streets began to resume their usual appearance. The activity crushed by the pseudo republic was awakened. The painter and sculptor were in their studios; the workmen in their shops; the merchants of greater and less importance filled up their stock, and looked forward to a revival of business under the mild and beneficent rule which had so often saved Rome. Religion was again free. The clergy and religious moved through the streets; the churches began to be thronged with pious worshipers, the offices of religion were again celebrated with pomp. There were still, of course, men imbued with the spirit of the revolution, men who had joined in all the outrages, who looked with an evil eye on the French and on the clergy; and their old hate was shown occasionally in assassinations. But the reaction had set in and rapidly pervaded all classes. As has been well remarked: "Independently of the anxiety to behold once more that familiar countenance which never looked but with love upon the people, there was no class, no interest, no industry, that had not suffered from the wild and stormy period which, commencing with the flight to Gaeta, did not end till the Pope's Government was fully restored. To have him once more in his own palace was now the most anxious wish of his people; and this feeling was frequently expressed through deputations earnestly praying for his return."

The moment came at last. On the 4th of April, 1850, Pius IX. left Portici for his own city. Ferdinand, with his whole court, escorted him to the frontier. On parting with his august guest, the king knelt, with his son and successor, to ask a last blessing. "Oh, yes! yes!" exclaimed the Pope; "with all my heart I bless you, your family, and your kingdom. And would that I could express all my gratitude and that of the universal Church for the generous hospitality which I have received from you." "Most Holy Father," replied the king, "I have only done my duty as a Christian, and I shall thank God as long as I live for giving me the opportunity to fulfill it." "Yes," replied Pope Pius IX., "but your filial piety has been great and deep. Once more may God reward and bless you." Then he pressed the pious monarch to his heart.

The thought of what was then hidden, but is now before our eyes, rises to the mind. As faithful Poland and faithful Ireland seem in God's providence to be visited here with persecution, so all who befriended Pius IX. seem visited in this world with affliction at the hands of the enemies of the faith. We shall see, in the course of events, Pius receiving and consoling the dethroned King of Naples,

Queen of Spain, and Empress of France. Entering his own dominions as their sovereign, the Pope received a welcome all the more enthusiastic, as the people felt that reparation was to be made for the past. At every city on his route magnificent preparations were made for his reception. At Velletri the commander of the French army of occupation came to pay his homage.

His whole course from Portici to his arrival in Rome on the 12th of April was one triumph. Then, amid the thunder of cannon, the joyous ringing of bells, and hearty shouts of joy, the Pope entered the city by the St. John's gate, but entered it in tears. He had sought no earthly triumph, he had no ambition to gratify; but care and trial, weary days and anxious nights were before him.

Rome was in an ecstasy of joy; the Te Deum rolling up to the mighty dome of St. Peter's was caught up throughout the world; and a feeling of glad consolation filled all hearts. But the sovereign Pontiff, after receiving the official felicitations at St. John Lateran, and once more blessing the city and the people from the balcony, took up his residence at the Vatican, as one bowing to receive the cross.

Pius IX. signalized his return to Rome by an extension of the amnesty, and by the publication of a new indulgence in form of Jubilee. He had recovered his people, the real Roman people, and he wished all Catholics, to the uttermost parts of the world, to participate in his joy; he wished to see no clouded brows around him. He frequently repeated these noble words: "I return as a pastor, not as an avenger; *in urbem reversus pastor et non ultor.*" The traditional policy of the sovereign Pontiff, as well as his own tender piety, prompted Pius IX. thus to diffuse over the world, in prosperity as in adversity, the divine blessings of which the Vicar of Christ is the depository.

In his restored government the Pope selected, as his Secretary of State and Prime Minister, Cardinal Antonelli, who continued to discharge his important duties till his death in 1876. His court recalled names associated with the grandeurs of the Church: Monsignor Medici, of a family that had given several Popes, was Grand Master of the Palace; his Grand Chamberlain, Count Edward Borromeo, was of the family of Saint Charles; Pacca, Master of the Chamber, was a nephew of the famous cardinal of the name. The Count de Falloux, Prince Hohenlohe, Count Xavier de Merode, Talbot de Malahide, represented in his household, France, Germany, Belgium, and Ireland. He wished the whole world to be represented, also, in the Sacred College. When he ascended the Pontifical throne, only nine of the sixty-one living cardinals had been born beyond the limits of Italy. In his first promotion, after his return to the holy city, of the fourteen prelates honored by this dignity, only four were Italians; the rest were selected among the most eminent men of the Catholic world. The fourteen cardinals of this promotion were: Monsignor Figueredo, archbishop of Braga in Portugal; Monsignor Bonnel y Orbe, archbishop of Toledo, and Monsignor Romo, archbishop of Seville in Spain; Archbishop Geissel of Cologne, Bishop Sommerau Bekh, of Olmutz; Prince Bishop Doepenbrock, of Breslau in Germany; Archbishop Wiseman, of Westminster in England; Monsignor Cosenza, archbishop of Capua; Monsignor Pecci, Bishop of Gubbio, Monsignor Ferrari, Nuncio Apostolic at Paris, and Monsignor Roberti.

The appointment of an English cardinal was connected with one of the great works of the reign of Pius IX., the restoration of the hierarchy in England, crowning with the splendors of the Church the Catholic emancipation won by the zeal and perseverance of O'Connell, twenty years before. From the days of Elizabeth, when the last of the hierarchy founded by Augustine died, England in her Catholic children, had, amid trial and persecution, been governed by archpriests and then by Vicars Apostolic. Gregory XVI. had increased these in number to meet the increasing wants of the Church, which won earnest and humble Catholics by emigration from Ireland, and men of learning, zeal, and devotedness by conversions among the most cultured and noblest of England's sons. To the great mind of Pius, the moment seemed present when a regular hierarchy should be established. After consulting the English prelates and the College of Cardinals, the Pope, on the 29th of September, 1850, published the bull *Universalis Ecclesiæ*, by which the See of Westminster was erected, and the illustrious Nicholas Wiseman appointed its first archbishop. Twelve other sees as suffragans, constituted the new hierarchy. Pius IX. in carrying out his great work conformed to the spirit of the Emancipation Act, which, providing for such a step on the part of the sovereign Pontiff, forbade any Catholic bishop to assume as the title of his see the name of any actually filled by one adhering to the Church of England. The new sees were Westminster, the Metropolitan, Southwark, Hexham, Beverly, Liverpool, Salford, Shrewsbury, Newport, Clifton, Plymouth, Nottingham, Birmingham, and Northampton.

The hearts of the Catholics were filled with consolation and hope, on beholding the Church organized once more as fully as in the most Catholic countries, and the new archbishop raised almost immediately to the dignity of cardinal; but while it afforded consolation to their hearts, it roused a storm of fury in Protestant England that it is impossible to explain or describe. The press, ever eager to fan any excitement, teemed with articles on what was styled the Papal aggression. The clergy of the Established Church took up the alarm, and the pulpit echoed the cry, while charges and documents of all kinds were circulated among their flocks. Parliament even considered the question, and, to appease the popular fury, passed, on the 2d of August, 1851, a law which forbade any Catholic bishop in England or Ireland to take the title of his see. Fine and imprisonment awaited any one who, knowing of a violation of this law, neglected to denounce the offending bishop. The law was passed, although during the debate it was admitted that it could not be enforced.

In England the bishops and clergy did nothing to fan the popular outbreak

Relying on divine Providence to quell the tempest by a word, they sought by their zeal and devotion to their holy calling to show how little ground existed for the panic fears. An appeal to the English people, in all the grand and dignified language of Christian eloquence which Cardinal Wiseman could employ, was unheeded at the time; but in a few years wiser counsels prevailed. No prosecutions followed the constant violations of the law; the Church pursued its work among the poor and lowly, unchecked and undismayed; her bishops showed their fellow-citizens that they were as truly English and worthy of esteem, when called by an English title, as they had been when their titles were derived from some see in the parts of the infidels.

The opposition in England was noisy, but not attended with any real persecution. But there were other lands where the Pope had to deplore violence toward

the faithful bishops and people. New
Granada, led away by designing men under
the influence of secret societies, assailed
the liberties and rights of the
Church. Pope Pius IX. in 1847 had addressed
a kindly remonstrance to the
president of that republic, but this did
not check the course of anti-Catholic legislation.
In 1850, the seminary of Bogota
was confiscated; and the next year
the visitation of convents by the bishops
was prohibited; a law required the people
to elect the parish priests, while canons
were to be elected by the provincial councils;
the clergy were deprived of their
revenues, and the Congress assumed the
right of fixing their salaries and defining
their duties. We shall see the same idea
taken up in other parts. It is one of the
great schemes of the anti-Catholic revolution.
Men who do not belong to the
Catholic Church, and avowedly seek its
injury, hope in this way to weaken it and

break up its divine organization. They talk of justice and liberty! but are not Catholics entitled to justice and liberty, and should they be forced to accept fundamental changes in their Church, when neither clergy nor people desire them?

In New Granada the bishops and priests with one accord protested against the changes; they were imprisoned and exiled. The Vicar Capitular of Antioquia alone showed feebleness of mind; he yielded, but was severely rebuked by the sovereign Pontiff, who called upon him to suffer nobly with his brethren. The archbishop of Bogota, Señor Mosquera, and many of his suffragans were driven into exile, and the republic was almost deprived of bishops. The voice of the country was roused against the persecutors, and fearing a general outbreak the persecution gradually relaxed.

Germany showed another example of the world's war on the Church. With crime of every kind unrepressed, with secret societies unchecked in their efforts to undermine the very basis of civil society, governments turn all their energies to banish, imprison, thwart, and molest the ministers of the Church, whose whole vocation is to make men the best of citizens. The Grand Duchy of Baden claimed the right to appoint parish priests and other Catholic laborers in the ministry. The government even declared that Catholic seminarians must, before they could be ordained, undergo an examination before civil officials. Archbishop Vicary of Friburg, a venerable old man bending beneath the weight of eighty years, nobly opposed the absurd and tyrannical law. He was dragged before the courts and put under police supervision, like a criminal. His faithful priests were imprisoned, exiled, or fined. Catholic Germany was roused. Indifference could no longer prevail. Men had to come forward zealously for the Church, or turn openly against her. The great mass rallied around the standard of the Church. The bells and organs were silent in the House of God; before the general emotion, the government of Baden yielded, while Wurtemberg, Hesse Cassel, and Nassau, which had attempted a similar policy, halted in their evil course, and then the Catholics in those States enjoyed a season of peace, till Prussia once more disturbed the religious harmony that prevailed in Germany.

In countries that professed to be faithful to Catholicity Pius IX. found the struggle more difficult. Sardinia not only refused to recall the exiled bishop of Turin, but tore from his see the archbishop of Cagliari, and menaced many other bishops with the same fate. Supported by government, a professor in the Royal University of Turin attacked the Catholic doctrines, and publicly denied that matrimony was a sacrament. In vain did the Pope condemn his works. The Sardinian Government, arrayed against the Church, turned a deaf ear. It was preparing a law that assailed that sacrament. The king, with the usual subterfuge, accused the clergy of disloyalty and of making war on the monarchy. The Pope in a letter to the king put the question in its true light. "If by words provoking insubordination are meant the writings of the clergy against the proposed marriage law, we declare without indorsing the language which some may have adopted, that in opposing it the clergy simply did their duty. We write to your Majesty that the law is not Catholic. Now if the law is not Catholic, the clergy are bound to warn the faithful, even though by doing so they incur the greatest dangers. It is in the name of Jesus Christ, whose Vicar, though unworthy, we are, that we speak, and we tell your Majesty, in his sacred name not to sanction this law, which will be the source of a thousand disorders. We also beg your Majesty to put a check to the press which is constantly vomiting forth blasphemy and immorality. Your Majesty complains of the clergy; but these last years the clergy have been persistently outraged, mocked, calumniated, reviled, and derided by almost all the papers published in Piedmont."

But that State was given up entirely to the anti-Catholic war. Every year was to see it inflicting new wounds on the Church, causing new sorrows to the heart of Pius IX.

Goa, in Hindostan, the last remnant of the once mighty possessions of Portugal in the East, had been for several years the scene of a schism caused by claims of a right of patronage, set up by the Portuguese Government. To this deplorable state of affairs, so prejudicial to souls, Pius IX. put an end in 1851.

Spain offered another field for the care of the sovereign Pontiff. That kingdom, which had given the Church a Saint Isidore, a Saint Teresa, a Saint Ignatius, and a Francis Xavier, had, since 1832, groaned under anti-Catholic governments. Convents had been suppressed, religious orders banished, colleges and schools closed, libraries scattered to the winds, the property of the Church seized and sold, bishops' sees were vacant, and religion at the lowest ebb. Attempts made to restore Spain to the Church at last proved successful, and in 1851 Pius IX. concluded a concordat with Queen Isabella II., who in spite of her training showed a real and sincere love for the Church. Ecclesiastical property still unsold was to be restored; what had already passed to other hands was renounced forever. But while the good Pope could make this sacrifice, he stipulated in the most positive terms for the teaching of sound Catholic doctrine in the seminaries and public schools, under the supervision of the bishops.

Conventions with the republics of Guatemala and Costa Rica gave an impulse to religion in those portions of Central America; and in 1850 Pius IX. erected Episcopal sees at Basse Terre, Guadaloupe, as well as in Martinique and Reunion.

Holland next claimed his attention. There a schism had lasted for more than a century. A series of bishops of Utrecht had been appointed against the wishes of the Pope. In 1853, the Pope induced the King of Holland to allow sees to be established for his Catholic subjects, and Harlem, Herzogenbosch or Bois le Duc, Breda, and Roermonde became Episcopal sees. Here, as in England, there was an outburst of anti-Catholic feeling, for modern liberals have no liberality for the Church, and do not concede to the Catholics the right to manage their own affairs. But here, too, the excitement soon subsided.

The little body of Catholic Armenians who still clung to the chair of unity required more bishops to attend their scattered flock. Pius IX. established new bishops' sees.

America, too, claimed his care. The rapid progress of the faith in the United States required the erection of new sees, to give bishops in various parts where, but a few years before, the Church was scarcely known. Oregon became an archepiscopal see in the very year of the accession of Pius IX. In 1850, the Holy Father erected sees at Monterey, and Santa Fé, in the Spanish Mexican territory recently added to the United States, and in Savannah, Wheeling, St. Paul, and Nesqualy, and made the Indian Territory a vicariate under the charge of a bishop; three years later new sees were established at San Francisco, Brooklyn, Burlington, Covington, Erie, and Natchitoches.

France, with the Church full of activity and zeal, surrounded, however, by influences which, dating from the horrors of the last century, were deeply infidel, offered much consolation to the heart of the Pope; but the very zeal and energy of the Catholics in France led to extreme views and occasional dissensions, which threatened evil to the whole Catholic body, as the old Gallican feeling began to revive. This called forth from the Pope the encyclical *Inter Multiplices* addressed to the French bishops. He praised the bishops for their zeal in holding provincial councils and in restoring the Roman liturgy in dioceses where local ones had for a time prevailed, but he deplored the dissensions which prevailed. "If there ever was a time," he says, "when you should preserve among you concord of mind and will it is now, especially when the Catholic Church enjoys among you peace, liberty, and protection." He gave wise directions as to debated questions of the use of the Pagan classics in education, requiring them when used to be thoroughly freed of all that could contaminate the Catholic heart. He urged the bishops to favor with their encouragement the men who, versed in letters and science, and animated by the Catholic spirit, devoted their vigils to the composition of books and journals for the propagation and defense of the truth; but he cautions these writers to use their talents in all submission to the bishops whom Providence had appointed to direct, warn, and if necessary, censure them.

The words of the Holy Father restored peace and harmony. In Germany the Church, freed by the events of 1848, showed new life and vitality. God prepared it for a coming struggle, as yet but dimly seen. The bishops assembled and gained ground, addressing the Austrian, Prussian, and Bavarian Governments in favor of the liberties of the Church; the clergy gained many converts, the laity formed Catholic associations which took the name of Pius IX. As these grew, general congresses of their deputies met each year, and these assemblies addressed the Holy Father in words of devoted loyalty, and year by year he sent them his apostolical benediction, and to encourage them still more, granted special indulgences to the members.

But these partial graces did not satisfy the loving heart of Pius IX. In the space of twenty years he no less than eight times granted to the Catholic world a plenary indulgence in form of Jubilee. No previous Pope had ever so liberally drawn on the treasury of the Church. He felt that a war of opposition was at hand, and that it became him to arm his children with prayer.

Every one of these grants was induced by grave reasons. The first was issued according to custom, when he took possession of the Church of St. John Lateran. On the 25th of March, 1850, the Pope promulgated a second Jubilee to thank God for restoring the Pontifical throne, and to implore the Father of Mercies to still the fearful tempest that was sweeping over the globe,.to preserve his flock from the allurements of error, to confound heresies, increase faith, and grant the Church repose and peace. This Jubilee was to replace the usual solemn one that should have been announced at the commencement of the year.

On the 21st of November, 1851, in view of the great dangers that threatened the Church, he ordered public prayers in Rome, in order to appease the wrath of God, and directed the bishops throughout the world to have similar prayers offered. To stimulate the faithful to the holy ex-

MEDAL OF POPE PIUS IX, IN 1853.

ercise, he granted for a month a plenary indulgence in the form of a Jubilee.

Thus did the Holy Father spread throughout his immense flock the spirit of faith, of prayer, of union, of mutual charity, of zeal for the house of God, and a holy courage to meet all dangers and persecutions for the cause of God.

CHAPTER VIII.

THE DEFINITION OF THE DOGMA OF THE IMMACULATE CONCEPTION OF THE BLESSED VIRGIN MARY. — THE ACCIDENT AT THE CHURCH OF ST. AGNES. — "IMMACULATE VIRGIN, HELP US!"

EXILED at Gaeta, Pius IX. had, in letters addressed to the Catholic bishops throughout the world, requested a statement of the belief immemorially held in each diocese in regard to the Immaculate Conception of the Blessed Virgin Mary. Six hundred bishops, of all lands and tongues, attested that the bishops, clergy, and people had always believed that Mary was conceived without sin; that from the first moment of her existence she was by a special privilege preserved from the original sin which attached to all other descendants of Adam and Eve. The point, as one not decided, may have been debated in the schools, but in the Catholic heart and in Catholic devotion there was no doubt. Not only did these bishops give their testimony to this fact, but nine out of ten, in replying to the Holy Father, earnestly urged him to give a doctrinal definition, that would place the belief among the dogmas of the Church, previous decisions having so far paved the way that attacks on the doctrine had been absolutely forbidden. The plan adopted by Pope Pius IX. was possible only in our century, when communication with all parts of the world has become easy and rapid. This too made it easy for numbers of bishops to respond to the call of the Holy Father, when he summoned all the bishops who could do so to assist him on the solemn occasion. One hundred and ninety-two bishops repaired to Rome, representing the most widely-separated countries on earth. The Czar Nicholas of Russia alone thwarted the wishes of the Holy Father, by forbidding the Catholic bishops in his States to visit the holy city; and his opposition was all the more strange, as the Greek Church rivals the Latin in the honors which it pays to Mary.

The bishops thus gathered together, though not in a formal council, well represented the Universal Church. Cardinals like Patrizzi, Wiseman; archbishops and bishops like Fransoni of Turin, Reisach of Munich, Sibour of Paris, Bedini of Thebes, Hughes of New York, Kenrick of Baltimore, Dixon of Armagh, Mazenod of Marseilles, Bouvier of Mans, Malou of

Bruges, Dupanloup of Orleans, Ketteler of Mayence, were there to aid by their counsels the commission of cardinals and theologians appointed to prepare the Bull. Never had Rome, since the general council of 1215, beheld such a gathering of eminent bishops. Meanwhile the whole Catholic world was in prayer, according to the counsel of the sovereign Pontiff, to obtain from the Holy Ghost a decision favorable to the honor of God, the glory of the Blessed Virgin Mary, and the salvation of the Church militant.

The assembled bishops virtually decided the infallible authority of the Pope in defining. When the question rose whether the bishops were to assist the Holy Father as judges in defining the dogma, or whether it was to be the act of the supreme Pontiff alone, the bishops themselves, rising from their knees at the angelus, exclaimed, "Peter, teach us, confirm thy brethren."

The eighth of December, 1854, was a

glorious day for Rome. The whole city was full of pious joy; citizens and strangers from all lands hastened to the vast basilica of St. Peter, now too small to contain them all. At last the procession arrives; bishops in miter and cope, in the order of their age, were followed by the cardinals. The Holy Father with a brilliant group around him closed the imposing line, while the angels and saints were invoked in the litany to join the Church on earth in honoring the Queen of all Saints.

When he had taken his seat on his throne, Pius IX. received the obedience of the cardinals and bishops, and the Pontifical mass began. As the chant of the gospel, in Greek and in Latin, died away, Cardinal Macchi, dean of the College of Cardinals, with the deans of the archbishops and of the bishops present, and an archbishop of the Greek and one of the Armenian rite, advanced to the foot of the throne and petitioned the Holy Father, in the name of the Universal Church, to raise his apostolic voice and pronounce the dogmatic decree of the Immaculate Conception, a motive of joy and gladness to heaven and earth.

The Holy Father did not reply. He bowed his head, as if to convey an affirmative answer. Then rising from his throne, he intoned the Veni Creator Spiritus in a loud, firm voice that rang through the basilica. Once more he implored the light of the Holy Ghost. Bishops, priests, and people mingled their voices with the clear tones of the Father of the Faithful, and the sacred hymn swelled in echoes through the mighty nave.

At last silence fell, and the eyes of the hushed thousands were riveted on Pius IX. With a countenance transfigured by the solemnity of the act, he pronounced slowly, but in a mild, firm voice, the decisive words of the Bull Ineffabilis.

He first laid down the theological motives for the belief in the privilege of Mary; he then invoked the ancient and universal tradition, both in the East and West, the testimony of the religious orders, and the schools of theology, of the Holy Fathers and Councils, and finally the decisions of the Popes in earlier and later times. Then with deep emotion he proceeded: "After we had unceasingly, in humility and fasting, offered our own prayers and the public prayers of the Church to God the Father, through his Son, that he would deign to direct and confirm our mind, by the power of the Holy Ghost, and having implored the aid of the entire heavenly host, and invoked the Paraclete with sighs, and he thus inspiring to the honor of the Holy and Undivided Trinity, to the glory and adornment of the Virgin Mother of God, to the exaltation of the Catholic faith and the increase of the Catholic religion, by the authority of Jesus Christ, our Lord, of the Blessed Apostles, Peter and Paul—"

Here his voice trembled, and he stopped to wipe away the tears. While all full of awe hung on his words, he resumed, as if filled with enthusiasm:

"We declare, pronounce, and define that the doctrine which holds that the Blessed Virgin Mary, at the first instant of her conception, by a singular privilege and grace of Almighty God, in virtue of the merits of Jesus Christ, the Saviour of mankind, was preserved immaculate from all stain of original sin, has been revealed by God, and therefore should firmly and constantly be believed by all the faithful. Wherefore, if any shall dare, which God avert, to think otherwise than as it has been defined by us, let them know and understand that they are condemned by their own judgment, that they have suffered shipwreck of the faith, and have revolted from the unity of the Church."

Thousands of voices answered a glad "Amen, be it so," and at once the bells of St. Peter's and the cannon of St. Angelo proclaimed to the world, that the Immaculate Conception of the Blessed Virgin was defined as an article of faith. Then the solemn service continued after the formal acts of enrolling and attesting the Bull.

The day closed with unlimited rejoicings in Rome, and throughout the world the Bull, translated into all known languages, gave a new impulse to piety and devotion. Books explaining the new dogma were prepared by men of the greatest learning and eloquence; hymns of singular beauty sprang from the hearts of Catholic poets; sanctuaries, altars, monuments, statues, associations rose on all sides in honor of the Immaculate Conception of the Blessed Virgin, and devotion to Our Lady, which had been increasing already, now took such a new impulse that the unbelieving world around could not understand or explain this nineteenth century devotion to Mary, though they felt it gave new life to the Church.

A few months later, and an event occurred in which many a pious heart beheld an almost miraculous preservation of the life of the Pope, and this they ascribed to the Blessed Virgin Immaculate.

On the 12th of April, 1855, the fifth anniversary of his return to Rome from Gaeta, Pius IX. left the Quirinal at an early hour, and passing through the Via Nomentana, by the superb church of St. Agnes, reached the Porta Pia. Nearly five miles beyond that city gate the Pope's carriage stopped at a spot where new catacombs had recently been discovered on grounds belonging to the Propaganda, containing, among other venerated tombs, those of Saint Alexander I., Pope and martyr, and of the companions of his triumph. Surrounded by cardinals and other prelates, generals and high officials, the Pope was received with respect by the professors and pupils of the Propaganda assembled to honor his visit. Pius IX. entered the crypt and knelt in prayer before the sacred remains of his predecessor, who more than seventeen centuries before had sealed his faith with his blood. After threading the long corridors, he seated himself on the ancient throne of the chapel, which doubtless several of his predecessors had occupied; and from it addressed the scholars of the Propaganda, in a touching allocution on the noble career before them as heralds of the faith. Then, after a few words to the distinguished retinue, he drove back to the church of St. Agnes.

This sanctuary, rich in artistic beauties, is one of the most ancient churches in Rome, having been erected by the Emperor Constantine at the request of his daughter, on the spot where the body of the saint was found. After visiting the Blessed Sacrament and venerating the relics of the lamb-like virgin martyr, he entered the adjacent convent of canons regular of Lateran, where a frugal repast had been prepared for their august visitor. The Holy Father then repaired to the parlor, and the brilliant gathering of eminent personages enjoyed a cordial and animated conversation. Among those present were Archbishop Cullen of Dublin, and Bishop de Goesbrand of Burlington, while almost every Catholic country was represented. Just as the Pope was preparing to depart, the superiors of the Propaganda begged him to grant an audience to the scholars of that great seminary. Pius IX. consented with that charming affability peculiar to him, and resumed his seat on the arm-chair beneath a draped canopy. All eyes turned to the entrance, as more than a hundred young clerics came rapidly in. In an instant the floor gave way, and with a fearful crush all in the room disappeared amid a confused mass of furniture, stones, and plaster, from which rose a blinding cloud of dust. The beams had yielded, and the whole sank down nearly twenty feet.

The few inmates of the convent not in the room alone beheld the accident, but they stood rooted for some minutes to the spot, unable to think or to act. Suddenly the voice of the Pope was heard, the first to utter a word. It announced that he was safe and uninjured. Assistance came; the Holy Father was first extricated, safe, but full of care and anxiety as to the fate of all the eminent and illustrious men around him, and of the young levites on whom so many missions depended. While all kissed his hand or foot, or made anxious inquiries to be certain that he had escaped unharmed, he thought only of others, and urged the rapid extrication of all. He waited in the garden for the result. One after another was rescued, some bruised by the stones and beams, till the last of all was raised. Amid that crash, where it seemed impossible for so large a gathering all to escape with life, not one was even dangerously injured; all were safe. "It is a miracle," said the Pope. "Let us go and thank God." Escorted by his fellow-sufferers, and by those who had come up to rescue them, they entered the church, where the Holy Father, deeply affected, intoned the Te Deum, and gave the Benediction of the Blessed Sacrament.

"Virgin Immaculate, help us," burst instinctively from the lips of Pius IX. as he felt the treacherous floor give way, and Mary granted him a miraculous assistance. She proved once more her powerful intercession, by preserving her devoted servant and all his companions with him. The Pope, protected by the canopy, had not received the slightest bruise, and his confidence in the Blessed Virgin was unbounded. While they were rescuing the fallen, Archbishop Polding, of Sydney, approached the Holy Father and begged him with tears to give his apostolic blessing to the wounded, perhaps dying, students in the ruins. "I have confidence in the Virgin Immaculate," replied the Pope; "not one life will be lost." His pious confidence was not misplaced; all were soon completely cured of the slight bruises sustained.

As the sentries at the door had prevented all entrance from without, nothing was known of the accident. The Pope drove toward the Quirinal blessing the kneeling groups on the way, his face lighted up with gratitude. But the carriages that followed showed pale and anxious faces; cardinals and persons of rank were seen in their carriages giving their usual places to young ecclesiastics evidently injured.

The report of a great accident and a

wonderful deliverance spread like wildfire through Rome. The churches were crowded, the devotion of the Forty Hours was at once begun in Ara Cœli, and public prayers were offered for three days in all the churches of the city, while at St. Agnes a special service commemorated the miraculous event.

The interior of the church has since been richly restored by Pius IX., and in a square court before the church is a fresco representing the deliverance of the Holy Father.

The 12th of April has become a holiday for Rome, kept every year with deep and pious gratitude.

The Sardinian king, aspiring to dominate over the peninsula, eagerly took part with France and England in the war against Russia, and as one of the powers interested was admitted to the Congress of Paris, at the close of that struggle. The only question before the envoys of the different powers was the position of Turkey; but Count Cavour, with that deadly enmity of the Church which characterized all his policy, introduced the government of the Papal States, as a subject demanding the action of the great European powers. Lord Palmerston, who delighted in creating discord where he could, and Walewski, the representative of the old Carbonari now Napoleon III., supported the views of the Sardinian statesman. The plot was formed for depriving the Pope of a large part of his territory known as the Legations, and placing them under a viceroy, intending, of course, to make that personage a mere tool of Sardinia. Prussia alone remonstrated at that time against this attempt to excite a rebellion against Pius IX. To carry out their plan, however, documents and pamphlets against the temporal power of the Pope began to appear. The most conclusive answer to all these was a report made to

Napoleon III. by the Count de Rayneval, long French envoy at Rome. It covered the whole ground so completely that, though it was a serious work, the result of long experience and study, the French Government suppressed it. A few extracts will show how it refuted the charges made against the government of Pius IX.

"Every independent State is expected to suffice for itself, and to be able to maintain its internal security by its own forces. The Court of Rome is reproached with falling short of this reasonable expectation; the cause of its weakness is inquired into, and it is generally believed to be the discontent awakened among its subjects by a defective administration. The real cause of the weakness of the Pontifical Government is a much more complicated one, and is, in fact, connected with quite a different class of ideas; but it is a much more convenient and rapid mode of arriving at a conclusion to complain of the administration, rather than laboriously to interrogate the history and the tendencies of the Italian race. . . . . During the last two centuries the general prosperity of the Pontifical system, and the abundant resources which flowed to Rome from all parts of the world silenced complaint.

"It is a general opinion that the Pontifical administration is placed entirely in the hands of the priests. It is asserted that the priest, whose lot it is to defend the interests of heaven, understands nothing of the interests of earth. People are unwilling to believe that the ecclesiastics employed in the civil service by the Court of Rome have most frequently no sacerdotal character, and that, far from monopolizing the whole of the administration, they have but a small share in it, are in fact a minority. I have often asked ardent opponents of the Roman rule what was their estimate of the number of priests employed in the administration. In answer to my question the number was generally stated to be about three thousand. No credit was given to me when I showed, with the proofs in my hands, that, taking them altogether, the number did not exceed one hundred, and that half these so-called priests were not in orders. And yet it is upon surmises thus groundless that grave charges are based, which the public accepts as undeniable."

This memoir took up the whole administration of Pius IX.; the lightness of taxation; the small amount of public revenue taken for the support of the sovereign; the honorable course of the Pope in paying off the paper money issued, during his exile, by the revolutionary government; the introduction of revised codes of laws, gas, railroads, and telegraphs. It was, in fact, a triumphant, because calm and authentic defense of the government of Pius IX.

But in reality proof was not needed. The revolution had decreed that the Pope should be deprived of his States, and the different powers of Europe bowed obedience. Napoleon III. maintained, however, an outward respect; he begged Pius IX. to become the godfather of his son, to whom he hoped to leave his throne; a new bishopric was created, and a new metropolitan see established, and finally the chapter of St. Denis was revived at his request. All this lulled the faithful Catholics into a feeling of security.

But Pius IX. was not absorbed with the affairs of his States. As Pope he had for some years been negotiating with Austria, and on the 18th of August, 1855, signed a concordat with that empire, in which the freedom of the Church was fully recognized. "The Roman Pontiff having by divine right throughout the whole extent of the Church the primacy of honor and jurisdiction, mutual communication in what concerns spiritual things, and the ecclesiastical affairs of the bishops, clergy, and people with the Holy See, shall not be subjected to the necessity of obtaining a royal placet, but shall be entirely free."

The Pope, in an allocution in November, testified his joy at the happy result, which freed the Church from the shackles that Joseph II. in the last century imposed on the Church in Austria. In March, Pius IX. addressed a brief to the bishops of the empire to exhort them to profit by their independence, and to make every effort to stay the progress of indifferentism and rationalism in their dioceses.

But while Austria thus consoled him, the pious Pontiff beheld with regret that the anti-Catholic party in Spain still persisted in its hostile course, continuing to sell Church property, prohibiting the religious orders from receiving novices, and banishing several bishops from their dioceses. The course of the Spanish Government became so violent that the Pope was compelled to recall his nuncio.

Beyond the Atlantic the same spirit of infidelity, which has in this century been the bane of Spain, and reduced it to so low a grade among European nations, is steadily sapping the strength of the Spanish-American republics. Mexico especially showed the fruit of infidel books and masonic associations. There the Congress forbade monastic vows, exiled the Archbishop of Mexico, and imprisoned the Bishop of Michoacan. These acts of violence and violations of every true principle of human government were condemned by the Pope in 1855 and the following year. Three new sees in the United States were established by Pius IX. in 1857, to meet the increasing wants of the Church. Alton in Illinois, Fort Wayne in Indiana, and Marquette in Michigan, a city deriving its name from the zealous missionary who first explored the Mississippi River, became centers of new life for the Church.

In the year 1857 Pius IX. resolved to make a tour of his States. No better answer could be given to the charge that his government was unpopular. His reception at all points betokened the greatest enthusiasm, and though full liberty of expression was allowed, no real grievance was laid before him for redress.

He left Rome on the 4th of May, 1857, amid fervent prayers and solemn benedictions. The whole city seemed gathered in the streets and squares to wish him a safe and speedy return. On the second day he entered Spoleto, where he was so long known and loved. Rather as a pilgrim than as supreme Pontiff, he arrested his course at Assisi to pray at the tombs of St. Francis Seraph and St. Clare, while at Loretto his whole soul seemed to pour forth in prayer, as he entered the Santa Casa which he had visited years before as a despondent levite in the House of God, debarred apparently from the lowliest place, yet destined by Providence to the highest.

The Holy Father offered the sacrifice of the Mass in the home of Nazareth, that dwelling so miraculously preserved and removed. Pilgrims hastened to the altar, and many received communion from the hands of the Father of the Faithful, whom they soon beheld absorbed in prayer before the statue of Our Lady.

Passing by Ancona he reached Sinigaglia, which exulted to receive a Pope whom it could claim as one of its sons. He had already shown his affection for his birthplace by erecting and endowing three new parishes, a hospital for the sick and incurable, and a college which he committed to the Fathers of the Society of Jesus, whose course of studies made it rival the great universities.

Other cities of the Pontifical States

then welcomed the Pope-King, Pesaro, Rimini, Cesena, Imola, till he at last reached Bologna, next to Rome the most important city in his dominions. Here his reception was a splendid one. Missions had been preached in most of the churches, strangers flocked in, so that the population of seventy thousand was nearly doubled. The Holy Father lavished gifts on the city and left money to complete the noble church of St. Peter. The city, to show its veneration for the great Pope, bestowed upon him a palace, in which he resided during his three months' stay, and which has since been seized by Victor Emanuel, whose base mind could stoop to deprive an aged Pontiff of a residence which was the gift of a grateful people. Bologna also presented to Pius IX. a magnificent state coach, long employed by him on solemn occasions.

Pius IX. had thus traversed the Legations which the false Cavour had represented as writhing under the Papal yoke, and he did not traverse them as sovereigns generally do their States, on the wings of steam. His tour lasted four months. It was a continued triumph, as the press of Europe, the hireling of the revolution, was forced to admit. The Pope moved around among his people, often on foot; all could approach and address him freely. He stopped to visit churches, charitable institutions, factories, and workshops, to examine public improvements in the ports and on the roads. Petitions were presented to him, but it was not for the abolition of priestly rule; on the contrary they asked the restoration of the old order of things when cardinals and prelates were prefects.

Pius IX. was welcomed not only as a beloved sovereign, but as a saint. People already began to talk of extraordinary graces obtained through his prayers, of cures wrought by touching articles that he had worn. One day a mother, long disabled by sickness, made her way with her children through the crowd, and cried out, "I am a poor mother, and I am dying; my two children here lose all when they lose me; save me, restore me to life!" Pius IX. stopped deeply moved. "My dear child," said he, "unfortunately I am not what you imagine; I have no power to control disease; but I have a father's heart to console you, and I can give your soul one word of hope. My child, God is good, infinitely good. You do not perhaps pray enough. For nine days now address yourself to Him who is the Providence of the orphan and the mother. I will unite myself to you during that time, and I hope that Heaven will hear you. Let us begin at once." He stood absorbed in silent prayer, the woman kneeling before him, and all present in the same attitude.

The Pope was not a mere tourist. At

Bologna, he held a consistory on the 3d of August, at which several bishops were preconized. During his stay in that city many personages of royal rank hastened to render homage to the Pope.

The Archduke Maximilian, later known as the unfortunate Emperor of Mexico, then Austrian governor of Lombardy; Robert, Duke of Parma, and his mother, and the Duchess of Modena hastened to Bologna to offer their felicitations in person. The Court of Turin sent a delegate, who began to declare the attachment of his government to religion and the Church; but the Pope interrupted him, telling him sternly to drop the subject, or he would be forced to contradict him openly.

Yielding to the invitation of the Grand Duke of Tuscany and Duke of Modena, Pius IX. visited Ferrara, Modena, Florence, and Leghorn, his carriage in Tuscany being escorted by the Grand Duke and his sons. At Sienna, Pius IX. visited the home of St. Catharine, and touched with respect her books, writings, and instruments of penance, and prayed before her shrine in the Church of the Dominican Sisters.

His return to Rome was welcomed with the wildest enthusiasm. The authorities, escorted by a select body of troops, and followed by thousands, came out of the city to receive the Holy Father at the Ponte Molle, where Constantine gained his famous victory under the ensign of the Cross. The public rejoicings ended on the 8th of September, by the inauguration of the monument erected in the Piazza di Spagna, to commemorate the promulgation of the dogma of the Immaculate Conception. The noble column is crowned by a bronze statue of Our Lady, fourteen feet high, and was inaugurated by the Pope, surrounded by the cardinals and the Diplomatic Corps.

Soon after his return to Rome, Pius IX. issued a manifesto, expressing his satisfaction at the condition of his States, and the loyalty everywhere manifested toward him.

Soon after this an affair occurred which was greedily seized upon by the anti-Catholic agitators throughout the world, to inaugurate a series of attacks on the Pope. This was the Mortara affair. A law long established, forbade Jewish families to have Catholic servants, and ordained that when a Jewish child was, by the consent of the parents, or by means of Catholic servants illegally kept, baptized, and thus initiated into the body of the Catholic faithful, it should be brought up as a Catholic. The Mortara family at Bologna violated the law, and a Catholic nurse baptized a child, which was apparently at the point of death. Pius IX. allowed the law to take its course; the child was brought up as a Catholic, and in time became a priest.

CHAPTER IX.

The French War against Austria.—Its Results.—The Sardinians seize Bologna and incite the Legations to Revolt.—Duplicity of Napoleon III.—The Kingdom of Naples seized.—Victor Emmanuel annexes the Marches and Umbria.—A Papal Army under Lamoriciere attempts to uphold the Pope's Authority.—Castelfidardo.—Ancona Capitulates.—The Maronites of the Lebanon.—Conversions in Bulgaria.—Hostility of the French Government.—The Canonization of the Japanese Martyrs.

Terrified by the attempt of Orsini on his life, Napoleon III. at last resolved to support the revolutionary party in Italy, which, led by Sardinia, sought first to expel the Austrians from the peninsula. The Emperor of France thus allied himself to the enemies of the Holy See, and prepared the way for the sacrileges which were soon to follow. He did

THE ANCIENT MONUMENTS OF ROME.

not foresee the retribution; politically blind, he weakened Austria and enabled Prussia to obtain that mastery in Germany, which she used to drive Napoleon from his throne and grind France into the dust.

On the 1st of January, 1859, the Emperor Napoleon gave the first warning of war. Pamphlets and articles in French papers began to discuss the position of the Pope, and reproach him with being maintained in his States by foreign arms. Pius IX. silenced this by requesting in February that France and Austria should withdraw their troops. Neither country yielded to his request. Then in an encyclical, dated April 27, he called upon the hierarchy throughout the world to gather their flocks around the altars and beg God to send peace.

The French ministry declared that Napoleon III. was loyal to the Holy See, and would maintain all its rights; but the truth was soon seen. The Grand Duke of Tuscany and the Duchess of Parma were driven out by conspiracies formed by Sardinian ambassadors, and similar agencies began to plot in the Legations.

The young Emperor of Austria rushing unprepared into the war was defeated at Magenta and Solferino. Soon after the Austrian corps occupying Bologna, menaced by a French corps under Prince Napoleon, abandoned that city without any notification to the Pope. The French allowed the Sardinians to seize the city, and excite Perugia to revolt. The Papal troops marched upon Perugia and easily recovered it; but the revolutionists who had shed so much innocent blood denounced the movement on Perugia as a massacre. Having the press at their command, they spread far and wide their false and infamous charges against the Pope.

The defeat of Austria roused the sympathy of Germany, and Prussia saw that she might be compelled to aid her Catholic rival. She telegraphed to Napoleon III. to offer peace at once. Austria accepted the proposal and peace was made at Villafranca. Lombardy was given up to Sardinia, the Dukes of Tuscany, Modena, and Parma were restored, and an Italian Confederacy was formed under the honorary presidence of the Pope. The very men who had exhausted all arguments to show that the Pope ought not to rule over a small State, now actually proposed to place all Italy under his presidency. .

But, in fact, the whole was a delusion. Cavour, the Prime Minister of Sardinia, never intended these provisions to be more than a dead letter, and Napoleon, by allowing him to carry out his plans unchecked, showed that he approved them. The duchies were not restored to their rulers, but occupied by Sardinian troops, under whose command they voted in favor of annexation to Sardinia. The same course was adopted in the Papal States. Bologna was occupied by a Sardinian army; Austrians and French had been for years in possession of portions of the States of the Church, but had never attempted to excite the people to revolt against the Pope; yet from the first the Sardinians stimulated and encouraged disaffection. Bologna and Romagna established a provisional government, and declared the King of Sardinia dictator. France could by a word have checked this iniquitous course, but she stood silent. The army in Rome saw the Pope's territory torn from him, but made no effort to maintain the integrity of his States, although Pius IX., in his encyclical of June 18, 1859, formally called attention to the fact that, by the express declaration of Napoleon III., the mission of the French army of occupation was to uphold the temporal power of the Pope.

Encouraged by this the Legations, another portion of the Papal States, revolted in March, 1860, and demanded to be annexed to the kingdom of Sardinia. They were annexed by a royal decree issued on the 18th of March. Pius IX. excommunicated the authors and accomplices in this sacrilegious act.

Meanwhile, agents of Sardinia were busy in Naples exciting revolt; the firm Ferdinand II. died in May, 1859, and the next year an expedition, fitted out in Sardinia under Garibaldi, landed in Sicily and almost without striking a blow, wrested that island from Naples. Emboldened by success he crossed to the mainland, and entered Naples, where he was proclaimed dictator. The king, abandoned by his subjects and most of his army, retired to Gaeta. Here he made a long and gallant defense, but after some months abandoned it, and sought refuge with Pope Pius IX.

No sooner was Garibaldi installed in Naples than Cavour prepared to profit by his act. To unite Naples with the territories held by Sardinia, Umbria and the Marches were required. Again Sardinian envoys, unchecked by France, excited revolt. Pesaro, Montefeltro, Urbino, and even Sinigaglia, the birth-place of Pius IX., enriched by his liberalty, put an end to the Papal power, and called upon Victor Emmanuel.

The Pope, finding himself unsupported by France, had reorganized his army, and a small force under General Lamoriciere, who had won distinction in Algiers, attempted to uphold the authority of Pius IX. Pious and devoted men from all Catholic countries, men of the highest rank, came to enroll themselves in the army of the Pope. Victor Emmanuel saw that under such a General the Papal authority would be easily restored. By his orders a Sardinian army, ten times as great as that of the Pope, was put in motion, and, without declaration of war, or any formality, this force, under General Cialdini, on the 18th of September suddenly attacked Lamoriciere at Castelfidardo. The Papal army was prepared to prevent civil outbreaks, but not to cope with a foreign power. Taken unawares by such an attack in time of peace, Lamoriciere met the attack gallantly. Four times he led his brave little army against the strong position of the Sardinians, till, cut to pieces by the overpowering force of the enemy, he was forced at last to give up the unequal contest. He did not draw off, however, till the field was strewn with dead and wounded, the gallant General Pimodan lifeless among them.

Lamoriciere retired with the remnant of his force to Ancona. There he was besieged by sea and land, and for ten days held out till his guns were all dismounted, and his ammunition expended. Then he surrendered, and his troops, exposed to every insult, often massacred on the way, were marched beyond the frontiers. The Papal territory was at once annexed, and Victor Emmanuel, crossing to the territory of Naples, met Garibaldi and entering Naples with him, on the 26th of December, declared Naples and Sicily part of his kingdom. On the 17th of March, 1861, he assumed the title of King of Italy, and ten days after the so-called Italian Parliament proclaimed Rome the capital of the new kingdom, thus announcing their intention to wrest the Eternal City itself from the Pope. Thus was the treaty kept which had provided that the Pope was to preside over Confederate Italy!

One of the great actors in this sacrilege, the plotter in the cabinet of Victor Emmanuel against religion and its head, Count Camillo Cavour, did not live to enjoy his triumph. He was smitten by sudden death on the 6th of June.

Pius IX. had now only the city of Rome and its environs, the primitive domain of St. Peter. He was utterly helpless to maintain his authority. He could only express his profound grief in his allocutions and briefs, protest against the new usurpations, and pronounce the ecclesiastical penalties against the spoliators. He was unawed by their violence or power. He spoke with apostolic freedom.

In an allocution of September 28, 1860, he stigmatized in bold and deserved terms the treacherous attack at Castelfidardo, and the unworthy non-intervention of France. He soon after justified his brave but unfortunate army, and struck a medal to commemorate the day, a medal bearing a cross and the legend "*Pro Petri Sede*" —"For the See of Peter." In March, he refuted the arguments of those who urged that the Pope should accept accomplished facts, and not oppose the progress of liberalism. He showed that the real object of the usurpers was to destroy every principle of authority, to destroy every idea of right and justice. He showed that the accomplished facts were incompatible with every principle of equity and justice.

The position of the Pope excited the warmest sympathy among the faithful Catholics throughout the world.

But the sovereign Pontiff had other anxieties also. The Maronite Christians of Mount Lebanon and Damascus were disarmed by the Pashas and left to the mercy of the Druses in June, 1860. Several towns were completely destroyed, every male slaughtered, the women and girls to the number of seven thousand driven off as slaves. Pius IX., in a letter of July 29, expressed to the Patriarch of Antioch, and his suffragan bishops, the sorrow that filled his heart; even in his poverty he contributed to the relief of the suffering, and excited the faithful to charitable zeal.

Yet if, in one part of the Turkish empire, the Church was thus severely tried, a triumph awaited it in another. On the 30th of December, 1860, many bishops, priests, and laymen of Bulgaria in a body abjured the schism of Photius, and, in the name of a majority of the people, sent a solemn Act of Union to Rome. Pius IX. replied on the 29th of January, 1861; and having appointed Monsignor Sokolski their archbishop, consecrated him in the Sistine Chapel. The new pastor of the Bulgarians, after reciting aloud his profession of faith, said to the Holy Father: "It is your work, if being dead, we are restored to life; if being lost, we have been found again." But the pious Pope exclaimed: "These are the works of God. To thee, praise, benediction, eternal thanksgiving, O Jesus Christ! source of mercy, and of all consolation." The schismatics, alarmed at this defection, resorted to violence and intrigue; many faltered in their new faith; Archbishop Sokolski disappeared, and is thought to be a prisoner in Russia; even bishops wavered, but the Archbishop of Drama adhered to the faith amid every trial.

The period was peculiarly one when bishops of schismatic and heretical communions nobly renounced all worldly advantages to acknowledge the Primacy of the Holy See, at the very moment when, to mere human eyes, it seemed bereft of all power and greatness. Armenian, Chaldean, and Coptic bishops, the Protestant bishops of Malta and North Carolina, may be numbered among those who, like the wise men of old, came from the midst of error, to pay homage to our Lord, under the guidance of a heavenly light.

Victor Emmanuel had assumed the title

of King of Italy, and Cavour had declared that the territory wrested from the Pope would be held in defiance of all; he even declared the purpose to make Rome the capital.

Napoleon III. yielded to the revolution. He indorsed the act of Victor Emmanuel, by regulating the limits of the Pope's restricted territory, and thus sanctioned the policy of Cavour, which, if justifiable in regard to the provinces, would be equally so in regard to Rome. He acknowledged the new kingdom of Italy, and was the first continental power to do so. Others soon followed the example, and Victor Emmanuel, thus sustained, proceeded in his war on the Church, suppressing religious orders, imprisoning the clergy, dispersing academies and schools. The indignant protests of the Catholics exasperated the French Government into open hostility; but when Sardinia sent Garibaldi to excite fresh troubles, and secure

Rome, France was compelled to speak. Dreading French intervention, Victor Emmanuel ordered Cialdini to attack Garibaldi with the very troops intended originally to support him. The adventurer was wounded and captured at Aspromonte in August, 1862.

It was thus decided that France would permit no more of the Pope's territory to be wrested from him.

The position of Pius IX. was grand. Abandoned by men, even by his own subjects, who had enjoyed under him all the blessings of a good government, he appealed to the hearts of the true faithful throughout the world. The Church rallied around its menaced Head. Testimonials of attachment came from every clime. Pius IX. invited the bishops to attend a ceremony of canonization. Twenty-six martyrs, one an American by birth, had been put to death by the Japanese at Nagasaki in 1597. The greatest veneration had always been paid to these proto-martyrs of Japan, and miracles attested their influence with God. The cause of the Blessed Michael de Sanctis, a Trinitarian, a member of the Order for the Redemption of Captives, was also ready. The call of the Pope could not be obeyed in Italy. The government, which kept repeating Cavour's lying phrase, "A free Church in a free State," prohibited the bishops of Italy from attending a canonization at Rome. Ninety bishops protested against such a mockery of freedom. But the holy city beheld bishops gathering from every clime. Three hundred and twenty-three cardinals, patriarchs, archbishops, and bishops, more than four thousand priests, and a hundred thousand Catholic pilgrims gathered in Rome. Ships arrived at the mouth of Tiber, from France, Spain, and Italy, which seemed like floating chapels; poor parishes united to raise among them funds to enable the priest of one parish to reach Rome.

From the Feast of the Ascension to Whitsunday was one prolonged festival. On the 6th of June, Pius IX. preached himself, in the Sistine Chapel, in Latin and French, to an audience of four thousand priests, all that the building could hold. When he had given the Pontifical blessing, a priest exclaimed, in the words of the Litany, "*Oremus pro Pontifice nostro Pio*," "Let us pray for our Pontiff, Pius." The response rose from all, as from one: "The Lord preserve him, and give him life, and make him blessed upon earth, and deliver him not to the will of his enemies."

The canonization took place on the 8th of June, 1862. The great doors of St. Peter opened at five o'clock in the morning. Thousands spent the night awaiting the moment, and scarcely were the portals unclosed, when the nave of the mightiest

INTERIOR OF SAINT PETER's CHURCH AT ROME.

temple of earth was filled. Fine paintings hung around, representing scenes in the lives of the martyrs, and of the illustrious confessor; thousands of lights illumined the immense edifice, and added to the charm of the scene. At seven, the head of the grand procession appeared led .by the orphans, and students of the ecclesiastical seminaries. Behind them came the religious and secular clergy. The Holy Father appeared preceded by the banners of the saints to be canonized, bishops, archbishops, patriarchs, and cardinals. He was borne slowly along on the *sedia gestatoria*, holding a lighted taper, all kneeling as he passed, while the chanters of the Vatican intoned the " *Tu es Petrus,*" and as it died away in the distance, another group chanted the "*Ave Maris Stella.*"

Thus was the Pope borne, amid the thousands of faithful from every land the sun shines upon, to the high altar behind the tomb of St. Peter.

When the Holy Father had taken his seat upon his throne, and had received the obeisance of the cardinals and bishops, the consistorial advocate thrice petitioned him to permit the names of the glorious martyrs and the confessors to be inscribed in the catalogue of saints recognized by the Church.

After the third request Pius IX. read, in a distinct voice, the decree of canonization, and then intoned the Te Deum, which a thousand voices caught up. Surrounded by all the bishops, the Holy Father thereupon offered the Holy Sacrifice of the Mass.

The sovereign Pontiff had not invited the bishops of the world to Rome, simply to take part in this imposing ceremony, solemn as is the rite by which the Church crowns her long and strict process of canonization, the investigation into the life and virtues of the holy persons, for whom the private devotion of the faithful seeks this public recognition.

Pius IX. has ever sought to perform his great acts, with his brethren in the episcopate around him, supporting his arms, as it were, like another Moses, while he seeks from Heaven for his people victory over their enemies. His allocution to them June 9th, 1862, begins by casting a mournful glance over the principal errors of our unhappy century: infidelity, denial of the divine origin of the Church, the encroachments of the civil power, pantheism, and rationalism. He then referred to the wicked conspiracy, the impious hypocritical efforts by which the godless threaten to annihilate the temporal power of the Apostolic See. He thanked the bishops for their unanimous support of the necessity of the temporal power, and adjured all to continue to combat error, to divert their people from touching or perusing bad books and papers; to promote the sound education of the clergy, and the Christian training of youth. He closed by asking them, in a voice choked by emotion, to unite in imploring the Father of Mercies to extend a saving hand to Christian and civil society, and to restore peace to the Church.

The reply of the bishops was as memorable as the allocution. They affirmed positively the supreme doctrinal authority and the infallibility of the Roman Pontiff. "You are the master of sound doctrine; you are the center of unity; you are the rock, the very foundation of the Church, against which the gates of hell shall not prevail. When you speak, we hear the voice of Peter; when you decree, it is Jesus Christ whom we obey!". They recognized as distinctly the necessity of the temporal. "The sovereign Pontiff must be the subject, the guest even, of no prince." "We condemn the errors that you have condemned; we reprove the sacrileges, the violations of ecclesiastical immunity, and the other crimes against the See of Peter."

This address, read by Cardinal Mattei, was signed by all the bishops present in Rome. The bishops throughout Italy, who had been forbidden by government to attend it, all signed it at once, with a single exception. The Catholic world applauded the act of the bishops.

The moral effect of this manifestation was immense. The Catholic world joined with the faithful of Rome to affirm the rights of the Holy See, and the right of the Romans to claim the city as the capital of Catholic Christendom.

That the anti-Catholic government at Turin grew frenzied at all this only shows the great moral force of the manifestation. Such was the famous period of the canonization of the Japanese martyrs.

The ceremony of canonization is one of great pomp and publicity. In a less solemn form, Pius IX. had already, since his elevation to the See of Peter, beatified several servants of God, that is, permitted their public veneration in certain orders, or places, until such time as the Holy See, on further proof of miracles wrought by their intercession, should proceed to their canonization.

Thus in 1850, he beatified Peter Claver of the Society of Jesus, the Apostle of Carthagena in South America, and especially of the negro slaves; and also the Blessed Mariana de Paredes, known also as the Lily of Quito; in 1852 he beatified John de Britto, a martyr in India, John Grande, and the illustrious Paul of the Cross, the founder of the zealous and austere Order of Passionists; in 1853 he beatified the Holy French Shepherdess, Germaine Cousin, and the Jesuit Father Andrew Bobola, martyred by the Cossacks, and in 1861 John Leonardi.

Thus the holy persons, who were by his decision presented to the faithful as models and protectors, represented both

POPE PIUS IX, AND HIS MINISTRY.

sexes, and all lands from America to Japan—the tender virgin, the laborious missionary, the heroes of Christian charity, and the devoted martyr.

CHAPTER X.

The Polish Persecution.—Efforts of Pope Pius IX.—The Convention of September 15, 1864.—The Encyclical Quanta Cura and the Syllabus.—Prussia's Progress in Germany.—France Evacuates Rome.—The Centenary of St. Peter.—Canonization of the Martyrs of Gorcum.—Garibaldi renews his Attempts on Rome.—Bad Faith of the Sardinians. — The French return.—Mentana and the Defeat of Garibaldi.

The Catholics in Poland had been for years the object of a fearful persecution at the hands of the Russian Government. The priests in many parts were swept away by its order, and hurried off to Siberia; the people compelled to choose between apostasy and the same fate; every bishop in Poland was driven from his see; some to perish while hurried along by Cossack hordes. Every effort of the unfortunate Poles to escape from the horrible tyranny that has for a century crushed them down was visited on the Catholic clergy. The united Greeks, a body which had always clung to the See of Peter, had especially been the constant objects of Russian persecution; their sufferings never abated.

No eloquence could exaggerate the sufferings of these devoted Catholics, or the fearful cruelty of their persecutors. The Russian Government has persistently denied the facts, hoping to crush the truth amid the horrors of Siberia, from which few of the victims ever return. But truth is powerful and will prevail. Those who might think the Catholic accounts exaggerated, are chilled with horror when they read the plain, unvarnished accounts given in detail, in a British Blue Book, as the official reports in Parliament are called.

The cry of these suffering children reached day by day the ears of the Holy Father. He appealed, but appealed in vain, to the Russian Emperor. At length on the 26th of April, 1864, he exclaimed: "The blood of the weak and innocent cries for vengeance, before the throne of the Eternal, on those who shed it! Poor Poland! I intended not to speak till the next consistory, but I fear by longer silence to draw down the wrath of Heaven upon me, the chastisement denounced by the prophets, on those who allow iniquity. I feel inspired to condemn that sovereign whom I name not. That potentate, who falsely styles himself Eastern Catholic, and who is only a schismatic, cast out of the bosom of the true Church, that potentate persecutes and kills his Catholic subjects, and by his ferocious cruelty has driven them to insurrection. Under pretense of suppressing this insurrection, he extirpates Catholicity; he transports whole communities to frozen districts, where they are deprived of all religious succor; he replaces them by schismatic adventurers. He tears priests from their flocks, exiles them, condemns them to hard labor, or other degrading punishments. Happy those who could escape and now wander in foreign lands. This potentate, heterodox and schismatic as he is, has arrogated to himself a power which not even the Vicar of Jesus Christ possesses; he pretends to depose a Catholic bishop lawfully instituted by us. Madman! he knows not that a Catholic bishop, in his see or in the catacombs, is always one, and that his character is indelible." Pius IX. called upon all to pray for the persecuted Poles.

When in December, 1866, the Russian envoy, at an audience, not only denied the persecution, but charged that Catholicity and revolution were identical, Pius IX. dismissed him, and broke off all intercourse with a government which set truth at defiance.

In 1867 Alexander II. declared the Catholic diocese of Kaminieck abolished; the Pope could employ only the newspapers to inform the Catholics deprived of their bishop that the bishop of Zitomir was appointed administrator.

Look at the map of Siberia, find if you can the village of Tounka on the Irkout, in its deep, pestilential valley. Yet, in 1868, in this spot alone a hundred and fifty Polish priests were still alive, survivors of hundreds sent there, saying mass by stealth, forbidden to appeal to officer or emperor, deprived of every comfort, and yet from the Ural Mountains to Kamschatka there were hundreds of similar spots reeking with the blood of exiled Catholic priests.

Meanwhile, the conspiracy against the

independence of the Holy See progressed. Step by step Napoleon III. yielded to the demand of Sardinia. On the 15th of September, 1864, he concluded a convention with Victor Emmanuel in regard to the Pope; but the sovereign whose fate was thus decided was not even represented in the proceedings. Victor Emmanuel bound himself by oath not to attack the territory still in possession of the Holy See, and to assume the part of the Pontifical debt corresponding to the portion he had wrested from the Holy See. France then agreed to withdraw its army within two years. Napoleon III. thus promised to leave Pius IX. to his fate.

The Pope could not but foresee the result thus shadowed forth, and he seems prophetically to have seen its consummation associated with the saddest days that France had known, for when the convention was made known to Pius IX., his only remark was, "I pity France!"

But with the shadow of a great wrong thus announcing its coming, Pius IX. was still the great Pope. On the 8th of December, 1864, he published the Encyclical *Quanta Cura* condemning a host of erroneous doctrines which he had from time to time censured, and of which a summary, or syllabus, was appended. There was nothing new to Catholics in this; but when modern liberalism and infidelity were confronted by this mass of sound Catholic doctrine, which struck at some favorite crude theory of the time, all rose in arms. The Pope whose declining power made him but yesterday one of whom they spoke with a kind of pity, became suddenly the great enemy of human progress, a man of boundless power and influence. The Encyclical and Syllabus have ever since been an inexhaustible topic; generally misunderstood and misrepresented, few stopping to think that it is one thing to condemn a general proposition as false, and another thing to set forth which is the true doctrine; and that this is a series of condemnations of errors propagated among Catholics, which it was the duty of the Pope to condemn.

The first articles of the Syllabus, or summary of the principal errors of our time condemned in the Consistorial Allocutions, Encyclicals, and other Letters Apostolic of our Holy Father Pope Pius IX., refer to pantheism, naturalism, and absolute rationalism. The next to moderate rationalism, which claimed too much for human reason, or excluded revelation. Then the prevailing indifferentism and latitudinarian ideas of the day are condemned, which seek to make men believe that the existence of the true Church and adherence to it are unnecessary for salvation. The condemnation of socialism, communism, secret societies, the Bible societies, clerico-liberal societies is formally renewed. The next topic is a series of errors concerning the Church and its rights. The Syllabus in fact lays down that the Church is a true and perfect society, absolutely free, enjoying her own peculiar and constant rights, conferred upon her by her divine founder, and that it is not competent for the civil powers to define what the rights of the Church are, or the limits in which they shall be exercised. It lays down, moreover, that the Church in the exercise of its authority does not depend on the permission or consent of the civil government, and the episcopal power includes no part dependent on the State. The Pope in these decisions claimed that the Church had the powers to define what was the true religion; to restrict Catholic writers even in treating questions not absolutely defined as articles of faith; to employ force, to acquire and possess. The direct and indirect temporal power of the Church was affirmed, and the charge that the popes had usurped the rights of princes, or erred in defining faith or morals, was absolutely denied. From the principles thus laid down others flowed: the right of the Church in certain temporal affairs, as for instance in regard to marriage and the education of children, the right of the Pope to institute bishops without the consent of the State, and the right of the bishops to exercise jurisdiction independent of any such sanction, as well as to direct the ecclesiastical education of students for the priesthood. The idea of national churches, not subject to the Holy See, but guided by State authority, is condemned as utterly at variance with the very idea of the Church.

The assumption that the State had no limit to its power was denied by the Pope as distinctly as it was by American statesmen, who appealed to a higher law of right and wrong than the acts of legislatures, which can morally bind only when they do not contravene the laws of God, and are exercised within the limits essentially belonging to them. All State action attempting to define the duties of the Church in the teaching of faith, the administration of the sacraments, or the direction of conscience is a usurpation. The right of the State to regulate the education of Christian youth, to the exclusion of the Church, and still more the education of candidates for the priesthood, is explicitly denied. So many and strange were the false doctrines set afloat, that the Pope felt it necessary to condemn the proposition that kings and princes are exempt from the jurisdiction of the Church. The proposition that the absolute separation of Church and State was the only proper course was condemned. A number of errors on natural and Christian morals were next censured. The Pope maintained that human laws should conform to the law of God, and that they receive their power from God, and that the decision in regard to their conformity lies with the Church. Materialism, with the doctrine that places all man's happiness in material success, was held to be subversive of all sound principle; as was the theory that successful injustice becomes just as an accomplished fact.

The exaggerated idea of patriotism that would make it justify any crime committed under its impulse found no favor with the Church. A host of errors as to Christian marriage were condemned, and this all the more necessarily, as the action of many States sought to separate the contract of marriage from the sacrament, to exclude the Church from conferring that sacrament, or establishing the dispositions necessary for its due and valid reception.

The Pope denied dogmatically by these decisions that the compatibility of the temporal royalty of the Pope with the spiritual power was an open question among Catholics, or that it would conduce to the happiness and liberty of the Pope to deprive him of temporal power.

In regard to States which had always been deemed Catholic, the theory had been zealously propagated that it was no longer right to hold the Catholic Church as alone established; that all religions ought to be allowed full scope. This as a general principle universal in application was condemned.

The Syllabus closes with a reprobation of the proposition that the Roman Pontiff ought to adapt his policy and the Church to what is styled progress, liberalism, and modern civilization.

Such is the famous Syllabus. Few thoughtful men can read it and declare that they would maintain the contradictory propositions as sound principles of action.

It put in a distinct form, however, many Catholic doctrines, and removed doubts; but it excited by that very fact a host of opponents. All who wished to exalt the royal power, all who wished to make the Church the creature and slave of the State, all who wished to withdraw marriage and the education of the young from the influence of the religion of Jesus Christ, arrayed themselves against the Syllabus.

Napoleon III. forbade the publication of the Encyclical and Syllabus, and having thus put an end to the liberty of the press, in the name of liberty punished some of the bishops for reading it from their pulpits.

That Pius IX. in the Syllabus condemned the true liberty of the press, or maintained that Catholic States should prevent non-Catholic subjects from worshiping God according to the dictates of their conscience under all circumstances, was refuted by his own conduct in the government of his States. A line between true liberty and license was drawn by the Papal Government, and a similar distinction is found in many of the constitutions of the American States.

Napoleon, in thus striking at the principles of the Syllabus, no more acted for the best interests of France than he did in planning with Bismarck the further humiliation of Austria. The revolutionary party applauded both acts as steps in the great work of destroying Catholic influence in the world. Sadowa demolished the power of Austria, the last fragment of the old German empire, and that humbled empire yielded up Venice, which, ceded to France for form's sake, was at once transferred to the King of Sardinia, who then transferred to France the cradle of his house, Savoy. Prussia, eager to build up a great anti-Catholic power, and to reduce her Catholic population to a helpless minority, absorbed Hanover and nearly all the other smaller Protestant States in northern Germany. Thus did French influence under Napoleon III. complete the establishment of a great Protestant power in Germany which it began under Richelieu.

Pius IX. amid these wars and rumors of wars looked beyond the strife of European courts to his world-diffused flock. It was an age of martyrs. The empire of Anam, Tonquin, China, Borneo smoked with the blood of Christians; but his heart was gladdened by better hopes, for the Church in Ecuador, under Garcia Moreno, and in Hayti, and in Japan gave promise of rich harvests of good; though the King of Sardinia, Mexico, and New Granada continued the war on the Church.

The public acts of the Pope during this period were many and important. An encyclical to the Belgian bishops settled a long dispute; another to the prince bishop of Breslau led to the submission of the disciples of Gunther; an encyclical to the bish-

op of Fribourg defined various points as
to popular education; and the Pope wrote
to the Archbishop of Munich condemning the errors of the school of Döllinger,
which finally resulted in a schism.

He continued his great work, organizing
new vicariates in mission lands, erecting
sees where the progress of the faith justified it. He convoked a Plenary Council at
Baltimore in 1868, and at its suggestion
erected Episcopal sees at Columbus, Grass
Valley, Green Bay, Harrisburg, La Crosse,
Rochester, Scranton, St. Joseph, and Wil-
mington.

One day in the year 1866, it was the
6th of February, the Pope was laying the
corner-stone of a new church in Rome.
It was a church that typified the times;
it was to rise beside the English college
dedicated to God under the invocation of
St. Thomas of Canterbury, who contended,
even to the sacrifice of his life, for the
liberty of the Church against the unjust

usurpations of the civil power. Alluding to the Catholics who so rapidly increased in England, Pius IX. exclaimed: "The principal Church in England, abandoned by her own children, and unable to bear others, for she is exhausted and barren, asks who are these Christians whom she has not brought forth? They are born of the true spouse, of her who has clung to the Bridegroom, of the oldest which is at the same time the youngest Church, the only one that is eternally fruitful.

"Hail Holy Catholic Apostolic Roman Church, whose unworthy Vicar and Head I am! I rejoice to see thy sons spread over the face of the earth, in spite of hostile powers! O Holy Church, may those who know thee not flock beneath thy shadow!"

Freemasonry, as the chief secret society of the world, and the type of all others, had been constantly condemned by the Holy See. In the Consistory of September 25, 1865, Pius IX. condemned it in the most explicit terms, to remove all doubts and call back any Catholics who in good faith had been allured within those societies. The gentlemen who boast of being always on the square resorted to a strange argument. To counteract the teaching of the Pope they pretended that he had himself been a mason. The story started in Germany, and they thought that by putting the scene in America they would escape detection. They declared positively that Pius IX. had been received into a masonic lodge in Philadelphia, cited his discourses, and declared that a number of his autographs were preserved in the lodge. Unfortunately for the story Philadelphia is in the civilized world. People there could read and write. They examined and found that there was no masonic lodge in that city of the name given; they found that no lodge in Philadelphia had ever received John Mary Mastai;

they could find no trace of his ever having been there, as in fact he never was; that no lodge had any of his autograph letters; masons themselves attested that the whole was a pure invention. The slander thus refuted has been revived from time to time, but in later versions care is taken not to specify the lodge or city too distinctly.

Pius IX. has never been within the United States, but he has shown in many ways his attachment to our country, and his admiration of our institutions under which real religious freedom is enjoyed. The poor negro slave was in his eyes as worthy of his kindly attention as the most exalted. Hearing that a slave belonging to a Louisiana family desired to receive his blessing, he sent her a special letter of audience, and when she entered said: "Daughter, many persons of rank are waiting there, but I chose to see you first. You are little and mean in the eyes of the world; it depends on yourself to be very great in the eyes of God." After conversing with her for some time, he asked her whether she had much to bear. "Of course I have," she replied, "but since I have been confirmed, I have learned to accept all as the will of God." He exhorted her to persevere in this love of God, and blessed her, and with her, all her fellow-slaves.

Pius IX. showed constantly this love and condescension for the poor, not only in audiences, but in his visits to hospitals, and other charitable institutions, and in his excursions in the neighborhood of Rome. He could by a witty remark rebuke the pretensions of the great; but for the good hearts of his poor, however much their ideas or address might vary from the etiquette of the court, he had every indulgence.

The Prussian Minister von Arnim in 1867 drove up to the Vatican in a vehicle with but one horse. As this was against etiquette the guards on duty prevented his approach. Bismarck, when this was reported to Berlin, ordered von Arnim to lower the Prussian arms and leave Rome if he was not permitted to drive up with a single horse to the Pope's palace. Pius IX., however, learning the difficulty, addressed a note to von Arnim through Cardinal Antonelli, intimating that his Holiness, taking compassion on the difficulties of the Diplomatic Corps, hereafter authorized the representatives of the great powers to drive up with one animal of any kind. Heartily ashamed of the part he had played, von Arnim never showed the letter to his fellow diplomatists at Rome.

The year 1867 was a glorious one for Rome, the eighteenth centenary of the death of St. Peter, the first of the Popes. The day of St. Peter and St. Paul was to witness a grand spectacle. Though Paris was inviting all to her great Exposition, Rome drew together five hundred bishops, twenty thousand priests, and nearly half a million pilgrims of the laity, coming from all lands to honor, with hearts full of love and emotion, a line which could thus celebrate a succession of more than eighteen centuries.

From every land came rich offerings to the Holy Father, who distributed them lavishly in supporting the poorer bishops, or extending the missions in distant countries. The concourse of bishops, and priests gave new lustre to all the festivals of the month. The procession on Corpus Christi, which fell on the 20th of June, was a prelude to the centenary. Half the whole body of bishops surrounded the Pope as he held the Blessed Sacrament in his hands, amid an assemblage such as has rarely been gathered together on earth, yet all so overcome by holy awe, that amid the universal silence no sound was heard but the falling of the water in the fountains without.

The next day was devoted to the commemoration of the twenty-first anniversary of the coronation of Pius IX. On the 23d the church of St. Mary of the Angels, at the baths of Diocletian, which the Pope had completely restored, was consecrated. The following day he officiated at St. John Lateran, and on issuing from that venerable pile gave his blessing to the immense multitude who filled the whole square.

On the 25th Pius IX. gave the hat to the Cardinal Archbishop of Seville, and made an announcement to the assembled bishops which was unexpected at that grave crisis, when Rome was menaced by the open hostility of the bands of Garibaldi, and the secret machinations of the Sardinians. But the courage and confidence of Pius IX. did not falter. He announced the speedy convocation of an

Œcumenical Council. The joy at this tidings was manifested by applause, and as it spread it filled the Catholic world with holy joy and interest.

The day of the Centenary of St. Peter, June 29th, 1867, Pius IX. celebrated High Mass in the great church dedicated to the Prince of the Apostles, and reared above his tomb. Eighteen centuries before, Nero, as the arch-enemy of the Catholic Church, thought to crush it by crucifying the head, the Vicar of the Crucified; but after all the vicissitudes of those long ages, the Church was still full of life, energy, though still pursued by enemies as bitter and unrelenting, and as blindly confident in their power to destroy her.

Pius IX. asked the Catholic world to begin the day of this glorious anniversary by supplication and prayers of thanksgivings. Then he proceeded to the solemn canonization. The Christian heroes who were thus placed on the altars of Christendom were the martyrs of Gorcum in Holland, nineteen holy religious put to death for the faith, in the mad attack on the Church in the sixteenth century; St. Peter de Arbues, assassinated in hatred of the faith at Saragossa; St. Josephat Kuncievicz, a Polish bishop who fell a victim to Russian fanaticism; and besides these martyrs two holy confessors, St. Paul of the Cross, the founder of the austere and laborious congregation of missionaries, the Passionists, and the Franciscan St. Leonard of Porto Maurizio, who as a missionary had traversed Italy reviving faith and piety. Two holy virgins, the French shepherdess St. Germaine Cousin, and St. Mary Francis of the Five Wounds, closed the list of those canonized in 1867.

The Centenary of St. Peter with its sacred festivals closed, so to say, on the 7th of July, when the Holy Father beatified two hundred and five Japanese martyrs, Catholic missionaries who had suffered for the faith during the terrible persecutions in that empire, some of them zealous men whom America can claim as their birth-place, or the scene of their previous labors.

Rome at the moment of this great solemnity was truly Rome of the Popes. The Emperor of France, according to his convention with Victor Emmanuel, had withdrawn his troops from Rome in December, 1866. Pius IX. maintained order in his States unsupported, and having but a small army under General Kanzler, made up in part by volunteers from various countries, chiefly men of rank and education, as well as of devotion and courage.

Yet Garibaldi and the revolution were at work. Victor Emmanuel pretended to exercise every diligence to prevent any attack on the Roman States; but an army was assembled and officered by Garibaldi, and transported openly by railroad.

In October bands invaded the Papal States on all sides; the city of Rome was full of their secret agents, who, under Monti and Tognetti, blew up the Serristori barracks, until then occupied by Papal Zouaves; all but twenty-seven, chiefly musicians, had been removed, but these perished in the ruins.

Sharp skirmishes took place all along the frontier at Monte Libretti, Nerola, Monte Rotondo; and an army under Cialdini was advancing, which did nothing to check Garibaldi, and was evidently intended to support him. General Kanzler resolved to act decisively and attack Garibaldi's main position. That adventurer lay at Mentana with ten or twelve thousand men in wooded hills. Kanzler moved upon him with a force of only three thousand men, November 3, 1867. France, roused at last by the invasion of the

Papal territory, and the utter violation of the convention on the part of Victor Emmanuel, had once more sent troops to aid the Pope. General Failly landed at Civita Vecchia, October 29th, and two thousand of his force followed Kanzler. A headlong charge of the Papal troops under Colonel Charette forced the Garibaldians from hill to hill, till they made a stand at the Vigna Santucci. Even the presence of Garibaldi in a strong position could not arrest their flight. They rallied at last in the walls of Mentana; its strength for a time gave them breathing space; but a part of the French under Polhés appeared, and the Papal Zouaves having turned their flank, the whole force disbanded by night, having lost fully a thousand men, while the loss in the Papal troops was slight, and on the part of the French but two killed.

Rome was saved for the time. The wounded Garibaldians were cared for with all kindness, and, the danger past, Pius IX. again granted an amnesty to all who had been in complicity with the unscrupulous invaders. The crime of Monti and Tognetti was of too black a dye to be treated as an act of war. They were tried, condemned, and executed; Victor Emmanuel and his Chambers protested, conscious perhaps, that the men had acted by their orders; but they would certainly punish in the same way any who should blow up a barrack in Rome in 1877.

CHAPTER XI

The Golden Jubilee of Pius IX.—The Bull Æterni Patris Convoking the General Council.—The Council of the Vatican.

The victory at Mentana and the reoccupation of Rome by the French, checked for a season the open violence of the revolutionists. Catholics throughout the world felt that it was a time for more than a merely moral support, and the little army of the Pope was swelled by noble volunteers from all lands. Hungary, Galicia, France, Belgium, Catholic Germany, and even Canada sent their contingents and maintained them at Rome.

Pius IX. was thus in peace to pursue his work for the benefit of his people and of his world-wide flock. An agricultural school for poor boys, the *Vigna Pia*, was established near Rome and supported from his privy purse. There zealous Brothers of Mercy formed forsaken boys to become supports of the State, intelligent, industrious tillers of the soil.

As the year 1869 approached, the faithful, now familiar with the life and interested in all that concerned their beloved Pontiff, saw that he would, if God spared his life, soon celebrate the fiftieth anniversary of his elevation to the priesthood. It was a general desire that the Golden Jubilee should not be passed unnoticed.

Dioceses in all lands prepared to send delegations to felicitate the Pope on the auspicious event and express the joy of the Catholic world. Carried away by the general movement, all the sovereigns of Europe addressed autograph letters to Pius IX. bearing their congratulations, accompanied by rich gifts. One sovereign only stood aloof; felicitations and presents from him would indeed have been a mockery. While every part of Italy sent its words of devotion, the man who arrogated to himself the title of King of the Peninsula was mute.

The Forty Hours Devotion at the church of St. John Lateran, closed by the Pope in person surrounded by the Sacred College, ushered in the long-expected day. Rome was overflowing with pilgrims, and as Pius IX. passed through the densely crowded streets he was hailed with heartfelt greetings from his people and his children from afar.

It would have been his own choice to offer his anniversary mass in the humble church near the Tata Giovanni, where he had for the first time fulfilled that exalted ministry; but St. Peter's claimed him, and even that mightiest of temples was too small for so grand a celebration. At eight o'clock, he celebrated a low mass at the high altar, beneath the bronzed canopy and the vast dome. Hundreds of the faithful who had sought with zeal the consoling privilege, then received holy communion at his hands. When the mass was ended Pius IX. gave his Apostolic Benediction, and in his clear voice intoned the *Te Deum*. It was taken up by all within the sanctuary, but soon the mighty host joined in, and the noble hymn swelled and rolled like the voice of thunders beneath the dome and arches.

In the evening of his Golden Jubilee, Pius IX. received at St. Peter's two thousand representatives of all countries of the world, the first felicitation being offered by Prince Charles von Loewenstein as the orator of the Germans, delivering an address signed by more than a million of Catholics, and accompanied by the richest offerings. Pius IX., deeply affected, replied in words of gratitude and joy to these expressions of attachment; but when they followed one after another he exclaimed, "My God, spare me, this is over-much happiness! I fear that soon when I shall appear before thy justice, thou wilt say, 'Thou hast received thy reward on earth.' No! not to me, but to thee, O my God, to thee alone, be the love of Christians."

The numerous presents and addresses were arranged artistically in the chambers of the Vatican, and the Pope, as he passed, regarding them, exclaimed, "I have my Universal Exposition too; not the product of my industry, but of the love of my children;" and pointing to the addresses of devotedness, he added, "There is the real expression of Universal Catholic Suffrage."

Rome had seldom enjoyed a day of such pure exultation as the Golden Jubilee of Pius IX.

The next day he made himself little with his little ones, by visiting his beloved spot, the Tata Giovanni, gratifying his own piety and the devotion of the forsaken ones whom it shelters.

Pius IX. signalized the day as king by granting an amnesty; as Pope by granting an indulgence in form of Jubilee for all who prayed for the Pope's intention, till he had carried it into effect by convoking a General Council.

The necessity of this important step, as a remedy to the growing evils of the times, which struck at all religion, all ministry of the Word, and mysteries of God, at all political, social and family ties, had occupied the mind of the Pope from the period of his seclusion at Gaeta. On his return he appointed a commission of fourteen cardinals to consider the question in all its bearings; each, with a learned theologian, being directed to elaborate a programme for the Council. "Then," said he, " we must pray, we must pray fervently, we must pray perseveringly that the Holy Ghost may enlighten us."

When the result of their deliberations and prayers was submitted to the Holy Father, he decided that the times called for the immediate convocation of the Council. This he announced informally to some of the bishops assembled at the Centenary of St. Peter. On the next anniversary of the feast of that Holy Apostle, he had issued the Bull *Æterni Patris*. In this great document he convoked a General Council to be held in the illustrious city of Rome, and in the Vatican basilica on the 8th of December, 1869, the Feast of the Immaculate Conception of the Blessed Virgin. He further declared it his will and ordinance that his venerable brethren the patriarchs, archbishops, and bishops entitled to sit and deliberate in General Councils should attend, unless retained by some impediment, which they were to report to the body in session.

"We hope that God, who holds the hearts of men in his hand, will listen favorably to our desires, and will grant, in his unspeakable mercy, that, acknowledging more and more the great blessings that flow abundantly from the Catholic Church on human society, and that this Church is the most solid foundation of empires and kingdoms, the sovereigns and heads of all nations, especially the Catholic princes, will not only not prevent our venerable brethren already mentioned; but will also be pleased to favor, aid, and assist them, with the greatest zeal, in all that can contribute to the greatest glory of God, and the good of the Council."

The State in modern times had so completely severed its interests from those of the Church, that the Pope after full deliberation concluded not to invite any monarch to send representatives to the Council. Some, indeed, possessed with that constant desire of intermeddling in the affairs of the Church, wished to protest; but no sovereign, except the Emperor of Russia, prevented the Catholic bishops in his States from freely attending the Council of the Vatican.

It was to be an Œcumenical Council. A great body of Greeks, Syrians, Armenians, Copts, and other Orientals, whose hierarchy was of apostolic origin, who had retained the holy sacrifice of the mass, the seven sacraments, and most of the doctrines of the Church, had been for centuries cut off from unity and the See of Peter, by schisms fomented in ages past by ambitious princes and bishops. To meet the errors of the time these churches would gain new strength by union. Pius IX., on the 8th of September, addressed these Eastern bishops: "We conjure and beseech you, with all the ardor we can infuse into our words, to come to the General Assembly of the bishops of the West and of the whole world, as your fathers did to the Second Council of Lyons and the Council of Florence, that, renewing the laws of ancient charity and restoring to vigor the peace of former ages, of the fruit whereof time has deprived us, we may, after a too long period of division, behold the pure and bright daydawn of that union arise which we desire."

Many of the Oriental bishops desired to attend, but the schismatic patriarch of Constantinople refused even to receive the letter; and though the Armenian patriarch promised to repair to the Council, he never appeared. The Oriental non-united churches, under the sway of Russian and Mohammedan, rejected or neglected the call.

The various Protestant denominations, which, with every variety of creed and worship, had arisen among those who in the sixteenth century abandoned the Latin Church, were further removed from the doctrine, worship, and discipline of the Church. They had thrown aside the apostolic succession, had no legitimate bishops who could be invited, they had no altar, no priesthood, no sacraments. But as many great and sincere men had come from those communities to find peace and consolation in the Catholic Church, and labor for its progress, Pius IX. addressed them also to induce them to examine seriously whether they were in the truth, and in the way of salvation. The invitation was not altogether unheeded. Though many treated the appeal with little respect, others in a spirit of calmness replied, endeavoring to justify, by such arguments as they could adduce, the original separation from the Church and their actual belief. Some, like the notorious Dr. Cumming, wished to be allowed to attend the Council and present arguments in favor of the Protestant doctrines, but the answer was one that could come only from an infallible Church. Questions that had been decided were not to be discussed. In the Catholic Church once a point of doctrine is raised and decided, it is decided forever. It is not a Church blown about by every wind of doctrine, accepting one system to-day, and another to-morrow. But the Pope offered to assign commissions of theologians who would receive any delegations from Protestant bodies, and consider their claims and objections.

The world was soon agitated by questions as to the Council. Governments hostile before, made it a pretext for fresh injustice, others weakly yielded. Austria nullified the Concordat of 1855; Spain, undergoing a new revolution, attempted to delude an oppressed people by new vexations of the Church. Russia continued her course of persecution, and in Poland especially the Catholics were in a position of the greatest suffering. In Italy the policy of violence and dissimulation still prevailed. All these evils formed the subject of an allocution of the Pope, on the 21st of June, 1869.

A private affliction befell him about the same time. In 1858 he had lost his brother Joseph, and now in the summer of 1869 he was deprived of his eldest brother, Count Gabriel Mastai. When the news came he retired apart to indulge in the grief which overwhelmed his affectionate heart; then he appealed to the mercy of God for his brother, ascending on his knees the Scalasancta, and offering the holy sacrifice of the mass.

PAUL III. (ALEXANDER FARNESE.)
Born February 28, 1468.
Reigned 1534–1549.

As the summer passed away active preparations were made for the holding of the Council. Five committees of theologians from various countries of Europe and America, who had been maturely studying the questions likely to come up before the Council, now printed dissertations and essays for the private use of the bishops, to aid in expediting discussions and debates. The north arm of the transept of St. Peter's, that which stretches toward the Vatican palace, and is dedicated to Saints Processus and Martinianus, was inclosed, and fitted up for the use of the Council, and supplied with proper furniture; rooms were prepared for the use of the congregations, secretaries, and others who were to take part in the august assembly.

Letters apostolical, dated November 27th, laid down the order to be observed during the holding of the holy Œcumenical Council of the Vatican, and on the 2d of December, Pius IX., in a general congregation, before the first session, addressed an allocution to the bishops of the Catholic world assembled in Rome.

On the appointed day Rome was instinct with life. Thousands of the faithful pressed forward to the great church to witness a sight seen only once in centuries. The splendid carriage of the cardinal rolled by the more modest equipage of some poor missionary bishop. The great church began to fill, for it is said that at least seventy thousand people were present beneath its roof.

The solemn day was ushered in by the booming of the great bell of St. Peter's; the thousand bells of the churches, and the cannon of St. Angelo and the Aventine Fort joined in the thunderous announcement. The Church which had survived the Roman empire, which had withstood the barbarians, which the schism of the East and the great apostasy of the

GALA CARRIAGE ISSUING FROM SAINT PETER'S.

West had failed to shake, was about to meet in a General Council, one truly Œcumenical, for all parts of the known world were represented, and by a greater body of bishops than had ever before assembled. Since the days of the Council of Trent, which opened under Pope Paul III., in December, 1545, a period of more than three centuries, the world had not beheld a council of the whole Church.

The cardinals, archbishops, and bishops gathered at an early hour in the Vatican; then, robed in white copes and mitres, they passed to the great hall in front, and thence to the vestibule of St. Peter's to await the coming of Pius IX., the Sovereign Pontiff. He soon appeared; all knelt in prayer; the Pope intoned the *Veni Creator Spiritus* in his clear voice, and as the choir took it up, the procession moved back into the palace, and down the Scala Regia to the vestibule of St. Peter's. First came the cross, with burning lights and clouds of incense, then the long line of mitred abbots, bishops, archbishops, primates, and patriarchs, a glorious line, most of them men of age, their faces showing the lines of care, the impress of experience; all bishops in their very look. Italian, Greek, and German, Persian, Syrian, and Hungarian, Spanish and Copt, Irish and French, American, English, Chinese, Australian, a very world gathering. Then came the cardinals, the most venerable body in the world; but even they were forgotten, as the Holy Father appeared, borne in his curule chair, all kneeling as he passed. The unmitred heads of religious orders closed the line. All knelt in adoration before the Blessed Sacrament exposed on the high altar, and then the procession entered the transept beneath a doorway over which was a majestic painting of our Saviour, and the inscription, "Go, teach all nations. I am with you all days, even

VATICAN COUNCIL.

to the consummation of the world." The sovereign Pontiff took his seat, and ranged on either side were bishops to the number of more than six hundred. High mass was celebrated by Cardinal Patrizzi, after which Pius IX., in an allocution of great beauty and the deepest piety, opened the Council.

The great work of the sessions then began, Cardinals Reisach, de Lucca, Bizzari, Bilio, and Capalto being named as presidents of the general congregations, and Joseph Fessler, Bishop of St. Polten, Secretary; but Cardinal Reisach was then prostrated by illness and soon after expired, so that Cardinal de Angelis acted as first president.

Other bishops arrived from time to time, so that in all seven hundred and sixty-seven took part in the proceedings.

In the earlier congregations a constitution on the election of the Pope, the projected decrees on faith, discipline, and religious orders were taken up, and the schema on faith was discussed in various sessions till the 10th of January. That on discipline was then taken up and discussed till the 22d of February. The subject of the catechism next occupied the Council. On the 7th of March, a formula of the definition of the infallibility of the Pope was introduced. The discussion of this point showed the first great variance of opinion. France, Bavaria, and some other States evinced such hostility, that it was feared by some of the fathers that any attempt on the part of the Council to proceed to a definition might lead to a general persecution. Others feared that an absolute declaration on the point might render it more difficult than ever to win back the Oriental churches, and the members of the various Protestant bodies. As to the point itself there was scarcely a shade of difference; all recognized that the decisions of the Pope *ex cathedra* were final, appeals to a future Council from his decisions having been condemned long before the Council of Trent; those who refused to submit to Papal decisions on faith, like the Jansenists, had been cut off from the body of the Church, and no one in the Council dreamed of summoning their bishops to take part in the proceedings.

The great powers of the world began to show hostility. The Emperor of France, in January, 1870, announced his intention of preventing the publication of the decrees of the Council in that country. Under such circumstances more than ever did it become the Church of God to declare distinctly and beyond all doubt what was the deposit of faith. The Council could only reply, as the Apostles replied to the Jewish rulers, and as they would have replied to Tiberius, Herod, and the King of Persia, had those monarchs sought to control the doctrines of Christ, which they taught enlightened by the Holy Ghost.

The second public session had been held on the feast of the Epiphany. There Pius IX. made his profession of faith, followed by all the fathers of the Council. There were two subsequent public sessions, while the general congregations had no less than ninety meetings. In these bishops of all lands spoke freely and fully. The third solemn session of the Council was held on Low Sunday. The fathers there voted the first Constitution, entitled "Of the Catholic Faith." The result of the vote was unanimous. Thirty-four cardinals, nine patriarchs, eight primates, one hundred and seven archbishops, four hundred and fifty-seven bishops, twenty-two abbots, and twenty-three generals of orders taking part. The Holy Father from his throne immediately approved this first constitution; and in his address gave thanks for the peace and harmony which had attended their action, and would, he prayed, continue. This constitution exposes the chief errors by which modern society has made shipwreck of the faith, and in four chapters treats of God, Creator of all things, of revelation, faith, and reason. It ends with the canons, short summaries of the chief errors, and their condemnation.

The form was that employed by the Council of Trent, which is deemed perfect.

Then the fathers continued their labors and prayers.

The question in regard to the definition of the infallibility was more earnestly debated, in view of the opposition manifested by the civil power in Germany and France, and by the violent attacks made upon it by Döllinger and other Catholic professors in Germany.

On the 13th of June the decree was

put to a vote. Six hundred and one bishops answered, of whom four hundred and fifty-one voted in its favor, eighty-eight against it, and sixty-two gave a conditional vote. It remained only to promulgate this decision in a solemn session, but Pius IX. would not act precipitately. A month passed; war had broken out between France and Prussia in which all Europe might be involved.

The fourth solemn session was accordingly held on the 18th of July. After a mass of the Holy Ghost the Pope entered; the prayer *Adsumus, Domine Sancte Spiritus* with the litany was recited, and then the Dogmatic Constitution on the Church of Christ was read, and the vote of each member of the Council taken. Of those who had wished the matter deferred till a more seasonable occasion, some had now joined the majority, others were absent. Five hundred and thirty-three voted in its favor, two only voted against it; when the result was announced, the sovereign Pontiff rose wearing his mitre, and proclaimed and sanctioned by his supreme authority the decrees and canons of the first Dogmatic Constitution " on the Church of Christ," solemnly pronouncing the following words: "The decrees and canons, which are contained in the constitution just read, have pleased nearly all the fathers. And we, the Sacred Council approving, define it and them as read, and confirm them by our apostolic authority." Then he intoned the *Te Deum*.

Here for the time the labors of the Council terminated. The position of affairs made it necessary to suspend their labors for a season, but a great work had been accomplished. By declaring that the doctrinal decisions of the Holy See were absolutely obligatory without any subterfuge, it adopted the syllabus, and with Pius IX., proclaimed that liberalism, as he has defined it, is incompatible with sound philosophy and revealed doctrine.

Bishops had argued and voted against the definition; not a bishop refused to acknowledge the act of the Council. All promulgated the decrees in their dioceses. Such had not been the case after the Councils of Nice, Chalcedon, and Constantinople. After every great decision of past Councils a heresy took form, and bishops were drawn away. After that of the Vatican, Döllinger and his followers, aided by the whole power of the German Empire, set up the heresy of Old Catholicism in Germany, and Switzerland, but the new heresy could not win a single Catholic bishop to their uncertain creed.

Yet the words of opposition, freely used, led away a part of the Catholic Armenians, and a schism arose in that body. A spirit of discontent had already existed, many disputes arising in regard to the nomination of bishops. A constitution issued by the Pope on the 4th of July, 1867, had been seized upon by the mischievous to mislead many; the decrees of the Vatican Council gave them a new pretext. They revolted against their legitimate patriarch Hassoun; the Turkish Government, acting under the instigation of some of the Christian powers, banished the patriarch, and fifteen hundred schismatics were put in full possession of all the churches of the Catholic Armenians, who numbered a hundred thousand, the faithful being driven out by Turkish troops. After vainly endeavoring to recall them to their duty, Pius IX., on the 30th of March, 1870, was compelled to excommunicate these rebellious children.

The decrees of the Council of the Vatican were accepted without any opposition in the British Isles, France, Spain, Portugal, Belgium, Holland, Italy, and

America; but the opposition to them which had been announced before the meeting of the Council, and which had been maintained during the sitting of that august body, was now brought to a decisive point. Submission to the decrees of the Council, or open apostasy, was the only choice. Döllinger and some sixty professors and priests, with a few thousand followers, openly left the Church, declaring that the Council had altered the ancient faith. They assumed the name of Old Catholics. They would have died out as a mere sect had they not received the support of the Bavarian Government, and still more of the Prussian and German. These latter soon introduced a series of laws, worthy only of some savage race, under which bishops were fined, imprisoned, exiled, their clergy treated in the same way, religious orders banished, apostate priests forced upon Catholic congregations.

Switzerland, adopting the same ideas, passed similar laws, and began a similar persecution; but both in Germany and in Switzerland the so-called Old Catholics, with all the power of government to back them, failed to seduce the people. The apostates never succeeded in gathering more than a handful of hearers to attend their sacrilegious services.

CHAPTER XII.

VICTOR EMMANUEL INVADES THE PAPAL TERRITORY.—HE TAKES ROME WITH AN ARMY OF SIXTY THOUSAND MEN.—PIUS IX. A PRISONER.—HIS ENCYCLICAL DENOUNCING THE ACT.

ON the 17th of July, 1870, France declared war against Prussia; the power which Napoleon III. had helped to build up, was, he now began to see, a danger to France. Unwise, unprepared, unsustained by Providence, he rushed into the contest. Ten days later, his ambassador at Rome announced to Pope Pius IX. the immediate withdrawal of the French army of occupation. "It is time to pray," said Pius IX., "but all will end well." In vain the Holy Father endeavored to arrest the fatal war; addressing letters to Napoleon III. and William, offering his mediation, and exhorting them to peace. By the 6th of August the whole force had quitted the States of the Church. Thus no time was given to call upon any other power for aid, and Victor Emmanuel was constantly menacing Rome, and Prussia endeavoring to induce Garibaldi to renew his inroads.

While all seemed to forebode a gloomy future, Pius IX. moved abroad among his people, greeted on all sides by heartiest applause. By his order public prayers were offered to avert the danger which menaced the city, and the faithful flocked to St. Peter's to attend the services of the

Forty Hours' Devotion. On the 19th of September the Holy Father was seen ascending on his knees the Scala Sancta, that relic of the Passion of our Lord, absorbed in prayer, and in the contemplation of our Saviour's sufferings. It was the last time he appeared in public. Pius IX. then returned to the Vatican, from which he has not since issued.

Victor Emmanuel sent Count Ponza di San Martino to Rome to ask him to abandon his rights. Pius IX. interrupted him. "I am not a prophet nor the son of a prophet, but I can assure you that you will not remain at Rome. I hope to be able to die peacefully in Rome; if Providence decides otherwise, His holy will be done. But for you, I repeat it, you will not long enjoy the fruit of your violence." When the shameless envoy persisted, the Pope replied, "You are whitened sepulchres. I know you not, and cannot know you or in any way treat with you."

On the 12th, the Sardinian army to the number of sixty thousand, without a declaration of war, without the shadow of any wrong received, invaded the Papal territory in three divisions: Cadorna moving upon Civita Castellana; Bixio, the friend of Garibaldi, on Acquapendente, and Angioletti on Ceprano.

Against such a force the little Pontifical army of ten thousand men could not expect to hold the territory. After offering a momentary resistance at Civita Castellana, it fell back to defend Rome. That city was soon surrounded on all sides. Victor Emmanuel professed to come only to defend the Pope from his own people and the revolution. The Pope himself well expresses what ensues. Victor Emmanuel counted on an outbreak in Rome to justify his crime. "His army waited several days to witness demonstrations of the Roman spirit; but it was in vain. It is certain that they then went as far as they deemed seasonable to excite the people to some manifestation in favor of the aggressors. Many emissaries from the camp entered the city, and *vice versa;* among them, in the first rank, the Minister of a foreign power accredited to the Holy See (von Arnim, Minister of Prussia). This Minister, the true Achithophel of our day, spoke peace with his neighbor, and evil in his heart; he used language at the Vatican, the very reverse of what he employed at the enemy's camp."

Finding that the Roman people would give them no pretext, the invaders resolved to attack Rome.

A trumpeter advanced from the Sardinian army to demand the capitulation of the city. Pius IX. refused to surrender the capital. His heroic army prepared to resist the overpowering force; it could not hope to defend the city.

At five o'clock on the morning of September 20th, the hostile army opened the bombardment of the city, Bixio with the heaviest guns at the gate of St. Pancras; but the lighter cannon of the Pontifical army were so well handled, that they silenced Bixio's guns and drove him back. At the Porta Maggiore, General Kanzler's handful of men more than held Angioletti at bay. Cadorna himself was at the Porta Pia.

While shells were exploding in all directions in the streets of the city, the Diplomatic Corps waited upon the Pope; they found him at the altar calmly saying mass. When at its close they solicited an audience, he thanked them. He told them that, to save the honor of his troops, he had been forced to resist, and he called the representatives of the powers to witness the violence committed against his independence. His orders to General Kanzler had been, in fact, to hold out only till a breach was made in the walls. As this now seemed imminent, Pius IX. begged the foreign ambassadors to repair to the headquarters of the enemy, and obtain an honorable capitulation for his heroic soldiers.

At the Porta Pia Kanzler, with only eight smooth-bore guns on a crumbling wall, checked Cadorna, who with two full divisions of his army opened upon him with fifty-two rifled cannon. He even drove the Sardinians back some distance; but Cadorna, by advancing his sharp-shooters, was enabled to bring up his artillery again, and at ten o'clock effected a breach between the Porta Pia and the Porta Salaria.

Then General Kanzler obeyed his instructions. He raised the white flag. Rome capitulated.

The grief of the Pontifical troops, devoted Catholics who from all lands had left Rome to defend the Holy Father, was extreme. But there was no alternative. By the terms of the capitulation they were to be sent out of the country by the so-called Italian Government. But the Sardinians and the rabble who accompanied them treated these brave men with the utmost wantonness of cruelty and insult, murdering and maiming many of the unarmed officers and soldiers who had surrendered.

It has been made a stigma on the great Montcalm that he suffered English soldiers to be plundered and murdered by the Indians after the surrender of Fort William Henry; but modern liberalism could not find it worth its while to censure Cadorna for giving up his prisoners to the savages of his army.

. The great desire of the brave volunteers was to obtain a final audience of the Pope. It was deemed too great a trial for the deeply-afflicted Pontiff; but as the soldiers drawn up in the great Square of St. Peter's sadly bore this last disappointment, a shout of joy arose. A window had opened; Pius IX., awakened by the shouts of his faithful defenders, had come forth on the balcony. He extended his arms as though he wished to clasp them all to his heart; then he raised his hands and his eyes to heaven, and blessed the soldier's kneeling in tears before him. Once more he extended his arms and raised them to heaven. It was his last farewell.

Then the troops filed out and laid down their arms at the Porta San Pancrazio, before the Sardinian generals and the Prussian Ambassador to the Holy See, who ranged himself with them.

For some days the city was in a manner at the mercy of the scum which had accompanied the invading force, and which Cadorna took no steps to repress, the object being evidently to terrorize the people with a view to what was next in the plan laid out.

On the 2d of October, by order of Victor Emmanuel, an election was held to decide whether the city of Rome and the Papal States should remain independent, or be annexed to the so-called Kingdom of Italy. The invading army and all its camp-followers voted. The terrorized people of Rome dared not approach the polls. Though the city and States had at least a hundred and fifty thousand voters, the whole vote, even counting the invaders, was only forty thousand. This was enough. They declared Rome annexed by the will of the people.

A royal decree declared Rome and the Roman provinces an integral part of the Kingdom of Italy. A second article added: "The Sovereign Pontiff preserves his dignity, inviolability, and all the prerogatives of a sovereign." A third said: "A special law will sanction the conditions proper to guarantee, even by territorial franchises, the independence of the sovereign Pontiff and the free exercise of the spiritual authority of the Holy See."

Catholics in England, France, Spain, Ireland, America, in the thousand countries of the world, might ask how the King of Piedmont had acquired the power to grant to the sovereign Pontiff independence in the free exercise of his spiritual authority, or deprive him of it.

Pius IX. could only deplore in silence all this crime, violence, and hypocrisy. Abandoned by all the great powers of Europe, he could do nothing to save his people from the war now made upon their religion. The monster who came professing to defend the Holy See, began that work by seizing the religious houses and the property of the churches, by breaking up the educational establishments of the Church, and by favoring every system of error, in order to weaken and destroy the Catholic Church.

The further continuance of the Vatican Council became for the time impossible.

Pius IX. suspended it by his brief of October 20. A few bishops from remote countries, who had lingered at Rome in hopes to see it resume its sessions, gradually dispersed, bearing to their distant flocks the sad tidings that the house of God was in the hands of the infidel.

The heart of Christendom was moved. In October the Catholics of Germany repaired to the tomb of St. Boniface at Fulda, to pray, where their apostle lay, for the Holy Father. In all lands prayers rose up to the throne of God, and addresses were sent to Rome to console the tried and afflicted Pope, by the expression of their devotion and zeal. From Italy itself, where the devotion was clear and unmistakable, to the Indians of the Rocky Mountains in the west, and the Chinese in the east, the voice of Catholicity was unanimous.

On the 1st of November, Pius IX. addressed to all the bishops in communion with the Holy See an encyclical letter. He had it printed at Geneva, for he placed little confidence in the articles of Victor Emmanuel. That document guaranteed his spiritual independence, but no sooner did the allocution appear, than every paper publishing it was suppressed.

This encyclical traced summarily the hostile acts of the Piedmontese Government during the preceding eleven years. It refers to the allocutions, encyclicals, and briefs on the subject from the 1st of November, 1850, as exposing to this century and to posterity the wiles, the unworthy and skillful maneuvers that enabled that government to crush justice; the seizure of part of the territory in 1859; the treacherous attack on his army in 1860; the hypocrisy with which they pretended to seek only to restore the principles of morality and order, when in fact they allowed the diffusion of every form of unbelief and of vice, insulted and imprisoned the ministers of religion, and despised the very Head of the Church; then the constant endeavors by emissaries to excite the people of Rome and its vicinity to revolt, and when that failed, the letting loose on his frontiers of hordes of criminals and adventurers, aided by means supplied by the Sardinian Government, till God in his mercy arrested their cruelty by the valor of the little Pontifical army and the aid of France.

While his subjects were in profound peace, the King of Sardinia, taking the advantage of the disasters of France, suddenly invaded his remaining territory, and addressed him a letter, which the Pope justly describes as a long and lying tissue of words and phrases put forward as those of a devoted and Catholic son, who asked the Pope not to consider the overthrow of his temporal power an act of hostility, and begged him to renounce it voluntarily

PIUS VII. (Gregory Chiaramonti.)
Born August 14, 1742.
Reigned 1800–1823.

and trust to his promises, in order, according to the phrase of the day, to reconcile what they styled the wish of the Italians, with the supreme right and the free authority of the Roman Pontiff.

"As to the demands presented to us," says the Pope nobly, "we could not hesitate, and obeying the laws of duty and conscience, we followed the example of our predecessors, and especially of Pius VII. of happy memory, whose courageous words we shall here cite and borrow: "We remembered like Saint Ambrose that the holy man Naboth, owner of a vineyard, was requested in the king's name to give up his property, that the king might replace the vines by mean vegetables, and that he answered, 'Our Lord be merciful to me, that I give not the inheritance of my fathers to thee.' Far less do we deem ourselves permitted to give up the ancient and sacred inheritance, that temporal power of the Holy See, which an evident design of divine Providence has preserved for so many centuries to our predecessors the Roman Pontiffs, or to consent even tacitly that another should possess the capital of the Catholic world, to trouble and destroy the holy form of government which Jesus Christ left to his Church, and which the holy canons framed by the Spirit of God have organized, in order to substitute a contrary body opposed to the sacred canons and the evangelical precepts, and to introduce as is their wont a new order of things, manifestly tending to associate and confound together all sects and superstitions with the Catholic Church.

"Naboth defended his vineyard at the price of his blood. Can we, happen what may, not defend the rights and possessions of the holy Roman Church, to whose defense, within the limits of possibility, we bound ourselves by a solemn oath? Can we fail to maintain the liberty of the

Apostolic See, with which the liberty and unity of the universal Church is so intimately connected?

"As to the great fitness and necessity of this temporal power to assure the Supreme Head of the Church the secure and free exercise of the spiritual power which he received from God over the whole world, the present events, in default of the proofs, would suffice amply to prove." (Letters Apostolic, June 10, 1809.)

The Pope then refers to the attack made on Rome, without waiting even for his answer to the royal letter to reach the king, and the bombardment and capture of the city by order of one who had just solemnly protested his filial affection to the Pope and his fidelity to religion.

"Since that day," says Pius IX., "there have been accomplished things before our eyes which we cannot mention without exciting the indignation of all good men;

infamous books, full of falsehood, turpitude, and impiety are exposed for sale at low prices and scattered on all sides; hosts of papers published daily to corrupt the minds and morals, to degrade and calumniate religion, to excite public opinion against the sovereign Pontiff, and the Apostolic See; impure and disgraceful pictures, and works of the kind published to hold up to insult and ridicule sacred persons and things; honors and monuments accorded to those whom justice and the law had punished for their crimes; the ministers of the Church, against whom passions are excited, generally insulted, some even treacherously struck and wounded; many religious houses subjected to unjust search; our palace of the Quirinal violated; a cardinal of the holy Roman Church violently expelled from the apartments which he occupied; other ecclesiastics belonging to our household excluded from that edifice, and harassed by vexations;

laws and decrees passed that manifestly wound and suppress liberty, the immunity of property, and the rights of the Church of God; and all these evils, grave as they are, will, unless God raises some obstacle, become still worse. And yet our present condition prevents our applying any remedy, and thus makes us feel the captivity in which we are, and the absence of that full liberty, which the intrusive government in its lying statements assures the world it leaves us to exercise our Apostolic ministry."

He repeats again his resolution to retain and transmit all the rights of the Holy See to his successors, and stamps all the usurpation as null and illegal; he declares and protests before God and the whole Catholic world that he undergoes such a captivity that it is utterly impossible for him to exercise his pastoral authority with security, ease, and liberty.

This grand document closes with appeals to all to pray for the Church of God amid the evils come upon it, and especially for a speedy deliverance and the restoration of peace. It will ever remain as a record of the great wrongs perpetrated on Italy by an ambitious king, and the revolutionary ideas of which he is the instrument, as well as of the noble firmness of the great Pope, and his solemn protest in the name of God and Christianity

CHAPTER XIII.

The Prisoner of the Vatican.—The Law of Guarantees.—The Encyclical of May, 1871, condemning it.—Peter's Pence.—Its Employment.—The Years of Peter.—The Twenty-fifth Anniversary of his Election and Coronation.

The last remnant of the temporal power had been wrested from the Pope. His palaces, except the Vatican, were seized. Possession was taken of the Quirinal to

ENTRANCE TO THE CEMETERY OF SAINT CALIXTUS.

convert it into a residence for Victor Emmanuel. Convents, churches, hospitals even were seized for barracks, government offices, stables. Nothing was left to Pope Pius IX. but the little corvette, the *Immaculate Conception*, over which his flag still floated, and which, after cruising in the waters of Civita Vecchia, finally took refuge at Toulon. The Pope is indeed at the Vatican; but the so-called Italian government claims that palace, with its galleries and treasures of art, and even the archives of the Church. It is guarded by soldiers of Victor Emmanuel and watched by his police. The danger of the Pope appealing personally to his people was deemed so great that the guards without made the windows the dead line. Every one appearing conspicuously at a window found that he was at once covered by the rifles of the soldiery without.

Most of those who held office under the Pontifical government refused to take the oath of allegiance to the conqueror; the Marquis Cavalletti, Mayor of Rome, set the example, which magistrates, professors, librarians, directors of museums immediately followed. They were dispossessed to make room for brigands who had followed Garibaldi. The Roman Academy of Archæology, refusing to change its name from Pontifical to Royal, was dispersed. The mint was spared for a time, but finally stopped. Pius IX. believes in the sanctity of an oath. He could not authorize his officers to commit an act of perjury.

Victor Emmanuel, to palliate his conduct, passed in March, 1871, an act called the Law of Guarantees. It was not a compact with the Holy See, but a mere act of the so-called Italian legislature, which could be repealed at any day when there was a majority in favor of doing so. It therefore really guaranteed nothing. It was not like our constitutions, something above and beyond the ordinary will of the legislature. In point of fact it has been a farce, as every clause has been annulled virtually. The first article declared the person of the sovereign Pontiff sacred and inviolable; but his residence is surrounded by soldiers with loaded rifles, who would not permit him to show himself in public. Article 2 provides that any attempt against the person of the Holy Father, or provocation thereto shall be punished as similar offenses against the king. Yet mobs have denounced the Pope in opprobrious terms, carried him around in effigy, encouraging the vile to violence, and no one has ever been punished for it. The infidel press has teemed with libels upon him, and they remain unchecked. An annual provision of 3,225,000 lire, equal to about half a million of dollars, is assigned to the Pope; he has never received it, nor has it been paid. The Vatican and Lateran palaces and Castle Gandolfo, as well as the museums, libraries, are reserved to the

Pope, but declared inalienable. They are therefore not his.

Article 9 tells the Catholics of other countries that the so-called Italian government kindly consents that the Sovereign Pontiff be fully free to fulfill all the functions of his spiritual ministry, and to post up on the doors of the basilicas and churches of Rome all the acts of his said ministry. Yet, in fact, the police have repeatedly torn down encyclicals and other documents thus affixed. By article 15, bishops are not required to take the oath to the king; the exequatur and placet are abolished, but in fact bishops who do not take the oath and obtain the placet are deprived of their income. The 18th article confiscated in advance all ecclesiastical property under pretense of reorganizing, preserving, and administering it.

Pius IX. refused utterly to acknowledge the law, or to accept it as a compact. He declared it to be a law of hypocrisy and iniquity. The first and only time payment of the allowance was tendered to him he repulsed the draft and its bearer. "I need money, it is true. My children throughout the world bleed themselves, so to say, to meet my wants and the many other wants you create daily; but what you offer me is only part of my own property stolen from me; I will never accept it from you except as a restitution; I will never give you a signature which would seem to imply my acquiescence in the robbery."

By robbing the Pope of his possessions, depriving him of his temporal power, these men sought to abase the head of the Church, to plunge him into poverty, and make him a degraded outcast in the eyes of the world. Never were men more deceived. They recall the graphic picture in the book of Wisdom of the sinners awakening to their folly on the day of judgment. They too may cry: *Ergo er-*

ravimus! The possession of Rome has not enriched the kingdom of fraud and violence; its loss has not impoverished the Pope.

When the Sovereign Pontiff was seen to be a prisoner in the hands of his unrelenting enemies, and he had early in September, 1870, decided not to leave Rome, in hopes that his presence would be some check to the headlong course of evil, the whole Catholic world was moved. The old Peter's Pence of early days was revived. France took the lead: and the idea was generously followed in all lands. In every church throughout the world a collection is regularly made for the Holy Father. Pius IX., rejected by Italy as a prince, is the Pope of the whole world, and the whole Catholic world readily contributes to his support and the management of the Church.

"Providence daily works a great miracle for me, and this miracle is as clear as the sun to the whole world, for it is from the whole world it proceeds. I am deprived of everything, but my children support me. From all quarters they send to their Father, and ask no account, and this Father, who has no resource except their gifts, is assisted so abundantly, that he not only has enough for himself, whose personal wants are but trifling, but they enable him to display generosity and give in his turn."

The prisoner of the Vatican not only still pays the salaries of many of his old dispossessed officers, but even maintains on half or quarter pay a certain part of his old army. He also maintains his establishment for poor boys, "The Vigna Pia," and "The Tata Giovanni," from which the usurpers withdrew all the revenues, for the simple reason that it was so dear to Pius IX. He also supports many of the Catholic schools, which endeavor to make head against the irreligious or Godless schools introduced by the invaders.

Besides all this is the maintenance of the Sacred College, prelates, guards, the keeping of the museums, allowances to bishops in Italy, Switzerland, and Germany, exiled for the faith and deprived of all means. This all requires between six and seven millions of dollars a year, and it increases steadily as the older Italian bishops die. Means are required also to maintain the young seminarians, many of whom are forced into the army and others deprived of the institutions in which they were formerly trained. Wherever a good work appeals, the Pope gives freely.

In spite of these heavy burthens on the Sovereign Pastor, Pius IX. is enabled to act as king even in his captivity. He has executed several works of art or of public utility at Rome, he has completed the restoration of Sant Angelo in Peschiera, and the magnificent portico of Octavia.

When a commission of artists reported the ruinous condition of the tomb of his holy predecessor, Gregory VII., at Salerno, he restored it at his own expense, with the inscription engraved by order of that Pope himself: "I have loved justice and hated iniquity, and lo! I die in exile—Dilexi justitiam et odi iniquitatem, et ecce in exilio morior." He maintains at his own expense the famous mosaic workers of the Vatican, and keeps them employed. The specimens sent by the Holy Father to the Centennial Exposition in Philadelphia show all what these mosaics are; Pius IX. is still able to bestow them as royal gifts, admired and appreciated in all parts.

The governments stood aloof and saw the Supreme Pontiff robbed of the States so long the portion of the Church, and so necessary to his free action, yet the princes of the world could not but bow in reverence to the greatness of Pius IX. Even they came as pilgrims to him, and received gifts at his hands, paid for, we may say, by the contributions of the faithful in America, Ireland, Germany, and France.

Two of the Russian princes admitted to an audience with the Pope, were struck with the beauty of a magnificent mosaic table, the only rich piece in the simple chamber of him who is personally so poor and simple in his life. "You are preoccupied," said the Pope. They attempted to excuse themselves. "Ah! but you are," he said, "and I know why. You are astonished to see this fine table amid my poor furniture." The color in their cheeks showed that the Pope had guessed truly. "Well," said Pius IX., "I will explain it: this furniture is suited to me; it is mine. The mosaic table does not belong to me; since it pleases you, it is yours."

These guests were of the family of that Alexander II. whose hands are red with the blood of murdered Catholics!

The captivity of the Holy Father began September 20, 1870. On the feast of the Immaculate Conception in that year, all the Catholics of Italy were invited to offer up holy communion for the Pope. Never was a nobler manifestation of Christian sentiment given than on this general communion. The 8th of December was really Catholic Italy's day of prayer in favor of the See of Peter. Pius IX. had chosen this beloved feast to perform a great act of apostolic authority. He published in the greater basilicas the decree which declared St. Joseph, the fosterfather of our Lord, Patron of the Universal Church. The whole Catholic world, laymen, priests, bishops, and cardinals had often solicited this decree from the Sovereign Pontiff. The petitions were urgent during the sessions of the council. Now, when the evil days prevailed, Pius IX. yielded his assent. The world believes only in material progress, in material gains, in material goods. It wars on the spirit and the spiritual. What can be grander than the faith of Pius IX.! Amid all the onset of the world he constantly raises minds to heavenly things, he constantly endeavors to bring heaven and earth more closely together, to bring those who on earth seek to serve God, and save their souls and the souls of others, in concert with those who reign with him in glory. He seems like one raised far above our earth, seeking to raise all minds to heaven, catching like Moses and Elias some rays of the glory to console and encourage the disciples.

On the 15th of May, 1871, Pius IX. issued an encyclical in which he stigmatized with just severity the deceptive character of modern society. He protests nobly against the violence of which he is the victim; he thanks the bishops and the faithful for the tokens of fidelity which they constantly give him; and taking up the shallow and deceptive Law of Guarantees, by which the Italian government seeks to palliate its enormous crime, he unmasks all its duplicity, treachery, and vileness. This encyclical, couched in the boldest language, is a proof of the unconquered courage and unshaken firmness of Pius IX. The Catholic world regarded with noble pride its august head, while the enemies of the Church vented their hatred and their impotent wrath. They had hoped to crush Catholicity by seizing Rome and abasing the Pope. They gave new life and energy to the Church, and made Pius IX. a spectacle to angels and to men. *Ergo erravimus!*

A month later, amid all the tribulations, heaven granted to the great Pope and the whole Catholic world afflicted in his person, a consolation without precedent. On the 16th of June, 1871, Providence permitted Pius IX. to celebrate an anniversary which no one in the long line of Popes had been permitted to see. He reached and passed the years of Saint Peter's pontificate at Rome.

"Thou shalt not see the years of Peter" had been said of every Pope, and till Pius IX. not one had done so.

The chief of the Apostles spent two years in Rome and its vicinity; then presided over the church of Antioch for seven years. In 42 he made Rome the capital of the world, the central See of Christianity, and remained there till his death under Nero, in the year 67, having governed the Church from that city twenty-five years.

The anniversary of June 16, 1871, was not celebrated throughout the city of Rome with all the pomp that would have been displayed had it still been the great Catholic city and not a slave, with church and shrine profaned. The solemnities were confined to the basilicas of St. Peter and St. John Lateran, but the crowd of worshipers was overwhelming. All ranks

INTERIOR OF THE BASILICA OF SAINT MARY MAJOR AT ROME.

and ages were confounded in this manifestation of love to Pius IX. and supplication to God to succor him, and rescue him from the hands of his enemies.

The whole Catholic world was in concert with the Romans. From the rising to the setting sun masses and communions were offered for Peter in chains, as of old, in the days of Herod. The telegraph brought felicitations from all continents. The sovereigns of Europe, led by Queen Victoria, paid homage to Pius IX., few, very few, omitting to honor him. Deputations reached Rome, so that one day the Pope almost needed the gift of Pentecost: he spoke no less than twelve times, in Latin, French, Spanish, and Italian.

It will scarcely be credited that on this occasion of holy joy when the illustrious successor of Saint Peter was thus surrounded by his faithful children, the archenemy of the Church, the very man who had deprived him of all his possessions as Pontiff, sought to force his way into his august presence. Yet it was so: and doubtless it was only to delude the Catholic world, by making it appear that the Pope received him cordially and pardoned all he had done.

Victor Emmanuel sent General Bertole Viale to Cardinal Antonelli to ask when he might be received by his Holiness to offer him the congratulations of the king. The General did not even see that Cardinal; he was received and bowed out by his Eminence's secretary.

It was not his last attempt. Conscious that his whole conduct, weighed in the impartial scales of history, would be stamped with the deepest reprobation, he made another attempt in 1872, which we will here anticipate. In that year the weak Emperor of Brazil, another tool of anti-Catholic revolution and imprisoner of bishops, was in Rome. He shocked Catholic feeling by becoming the guest of

Victor Emmanuel before paying his homage to the oppressed Vicar of Christ. One morning the emperor presented himself at the Vatican while the Pope was saying mass. At its conclusion, Pius IX. was informed of the presence of the Emperor of Brazil, most unexpected at that early hour.

The Pope ordered him to be introduced. When he entered, Pius IX. asked: "What does your Majesty desire?" "I beg your Holiness not to call me Majesty, I am here simply Count of Alcantara." The Pope rejoined: "Well, my dear Count, what is your wish?" "Your Holiness, I come to beg you to permit me to present to you his Majesty, the King of Italy." At these words, the Holy Father rose, and with a look that startled the intermeddling emperor, exclaimed: "It is useless to address such language to me. Let the King of Piedmont abjure his wrong-doing, let him restore my States to me, and then I will see him. Not before."

Some affect to think the attitude of the Pope harsh and unforgiving. The Pope is by his oath but the depositary of power received from his predecessors to hand intact to the next Sovereign Pontiff. He cannot alienate his States or approve the violence to religion offered in them. To this he must always say: "Non possumus"—"We cannot."

By the convention made in September, 1864, between Victor Emmanuel and Napoleon III., Victor Emmanuel bound himself by oath, that if the Emperor would withdraw his troops from Rome, he would not only not attack the dominions of the Holy See, but would protect them against any other invaders. The Emperor withdrew his troops, and left the Pope unsupported until the massing of Garibaldi's forces, unchecked by Victor Emmanuel, showed that Victor Emmanuel had violated his oath. Napoleon III. finally withdrew the troops when there was no danger to the Pope except from Victor Emmanuel. The question then is whether Victor Emmanuel kept his oath. Leaving aside all questions of right, has he invaded the Pope's dominions or not? As long as France was strong enough to resent, in case of perjury, the promise was kept, evidently not because an oath was deemed binding, but because France could enforce it. The moment France was weakened, the fear vanished, the oath was broken. Victor Emmanuel swore he would not invade Rome, but would protect it against invaders. To keep his oath he should have stood beside General Kanzler to defend the Porta Pia. How can the Pope make terms with a king who is bound by no law of national comity, by no law of nations, not even by a solemn oath!

In view of all this, a high priest of the living God, who by his position is to rebuke the evil doer, be he king or beggar, cannot by word or deed countenance perjury and oppression.

How uneasy the crown of Italy sits on the head of the usurper was seen in 1877, when a mere change of ministry in France alarmed Italy and made it fear that the day of reckoning had come. The day must come, and the evil doers must live in constant dread of it.

Let us return to the glorious anniversary of the Pope on which this application of Victor Emmanuel cast the only shadow.

It is a long established rule in Rome to commemorate by monuments and medals all important events. The day celebrated seemed to the chapter of St. Peter's to deserve such a lasting memento. Above that ancient statue of St. Peter which in the days of Attila, Pope St. Leo cast from the fragments of the Capitoline Jove, they set a beautiful mosaic medallion of Pope Pius IX. supported by two bronze angels, the whole resting on a tablet of antique marble bearing this inscription:

PIO IX. PONT. MAX.
QVI PETRI ANNOS
IN PONTIFICATV ROMANO
VNVS ÆQVAVIT
CLERVS VATICANVS
SACRAM ORNAVIT SEDEM
XIV. KAL. QVINT. A MDCCCLXXI.*

CHAPTER XIV.

Victor Emmanuel in Rome.—Seizure of the Quirinal.—Devotion of the Romans to Pius IX.—Persecution of the Church in Germany and Switzerland.—The Sacred College.—An Irish Cardinal.—Persecution in Brazil, Russia, and Italy.—An American Cardinal.

The anniversary of Pope Pius IX. forced Victor Emmanuel to a step from

---

* To the Sovereign Pontiff Pius IX., who alone in his pontificate equalled the years of Peter, the Vatican clergy adorned this sacred seat June 16th, 1871.

which he had long shrunk with a sort of superstitious terror, for his faith has degenerated to a mere superstition; his evil counsellors showed him that he must make Rome his capital and residence, as in fact Pius IX. was really king in Rome, receiving the homage of all, the tribute of all hearts. Accordingly, on the 2d of July, 1871, Victor Emmanuel made his entry into Rome and installed himself in the Quirinal palace. His court, less scrupulous than he, adapted the palace of the Popes to their vain and frivolous pleasures, and attempted to be at home; but the attempt was vain. The triumphant anti-Catholic revolution had for years aspired to the possession of Rome, as the crown of all their desires. They had reached it by perjury, fraud, and violence; but what had they gained? They possessed only the palaces they occupied, the churches and convents they seized; streets almost as devoid of life as those ruined ones that recalled the memory of ancient Rome. It was a Dead Sea fruit that had tempted their eyes and turned to ashes on their lips. Time did not change the condition of affairs. Real Rome was to be found in the churches and in pilgrimages to the Vatican. Rich and poor, noble and plebeian shrank alike from the invader and his godless horde. The invaders felt it, as one of their papers exclaimed months after: "Italy is as much a stranger here as it was the first day. Rome does not resemble a friendly city, but a city constantly writhing under a prolonged military occupation which it bears impatiently." For once the revolution spoke truly.

Only a few days after Victor Emmanuel's entry, Pius IX. received in the Vatican a deputation from a Catholic Congress at Rome, who presented an address signed by more than twenty-seven thousand citizens of the Eternal City. With them he deplored the deluge of iniquity that had overflowed the city; and he announced his firm resolution to make no compromise. "I am weary of all this; and yet I am not disposed to lay down my arms, nor debase myself to make any compact with iniquity. I shall fulfill my duty to the end." The next month, in August, a deputation of the Roman nobility, headed by the Marquis Cavalletti, saluted the Pope as Pius the Great and offered him a throne of gold. Pius IX. declined both title and throne with firmness, and yet with all his wonted cheerfulness. "What! in my lifetime! I admire your imprudence. The Church to canonize her saints waits till they are dead, and long dead. Humanity should be in no greater haste to canonize her heroes, for so long as a man breathes, no one can aver that his heroism will not belie itself."

The violent seizure of Rome, and the desolating war between France and Prussia kept many from the Eternal City, and caused many others to forsake it. It gradually assumed the air of a plague-stricken capital. Grieved as the Holy Father was at the afflictions which he saw about to befall his faithful people, he put all his trust in God and urged all to prayer, to look for relief rather to heaven than to earth.

The year 1872 was for the Pope one of trial. He saw evil done before his eyes, but was unable to repress it. He could but express his grief to the faithful who from all parts of his States flocked to him, the brave and devoted women of Trastevere or those more exalted in the eyes of the world. On the twenty-sixth anniversary of his coronation, delegates of two hundred dioceses of Italy came to tender him their homage, and his heart expanded with love for the whole country. "I bless Italy, but not those who oppress and scandalize it; I bless that privileged land which has produced so many remarkable men, so many holy souls, so many models of piety, and may the blessing have power to destroy evil and deliver us from the woes and oppression that now crush us."

But it was not only the faithful who came to pay homage to the Pope. The prince and princess of Wales, the future rulers of England, sought an audience. Pius IX. could in all sincerity thank the son of Queen Victoria for the freedom which the Church enjoyed in his mother's possessions, a freedom employed by Catholics only to refute by their conduct the false accusations raised against the Church in other countries where real liberty is unknown, but tyranny rules in her name.

During the year 1872, Pius IX. established two new sees in the United States, Ogdensburg and Providence, having previously in 1870 given a bishop to Springfield, Massachusetts, and to St. Augustine, the most ancient city in the Republic.

The victory gained by Prussia over humbled France, and the establishment of a German empire under William I. were followed by an open persecution of the Catholics, evidently planned long before, but ascribed now to the Vatican Council, which it was pretended entirely had changed the constitution of the Catholic Church. The ministers of the emperor were encouraged by a few rationalist Catholics at Munich, high in favor with King Louis II., who had denounced the Vatican Council, refused to acknowledge it, and excited fears as to its action. They formed the sect calling themselves Old Catholics, and led Bismarck to believe that with support they would soon rally around them nearly all the Catholics in Germany in a new organization ready to blend with Protestants, and be a supple instrument in the hands of government. The Catholic bishops and clergy would join them heartily or readily submit, they asserted.

Six years have shown that the real bishops and priests of Germany remain faithful to Rome, with the great mass of the German Catholics; that the priests who joined the new heresy number only thirty, and their adherents scattered all over Germany only seventeen thousand. In Bonn, where the bishop of the new sect fixed his residence, he cannot gather a flock of a hundred and fifty out of a population of twenty-five thousand. The real Catholic bishops and clergy have not joined them spontaneously, and though Germany could overwhelm France by brute force, she has year after year wielded that brute force with all the severity of baffled hate, and has utterly failed to drive a single bishop, priest, or even German child out of the Catholic Church into the new heresy.

Bismarck himself called his series of laws a war on the Church. They began by expelling without any judicial form, and depriving of the right of citizenship, all the members of the Society of Jesus, and other orders which the law pretended were affiliated with the Jesuits. Many of these priests had been decorated for services rendered in the army during the late war. The May or Falk laws, as they are styled, from their author, then suppressed all the ecclesiastical seminaries, under pretense of training the aspirants to the priesthood to a higher scientific degree in the German universities, hotbeds of dissipation and rationalism. The laws then abolished the articles of the Prussian Constitution which guaranteed the rights of the various faiths; they gave the State the power to nominate to ecclesiastical functions, and forbade bishops to exclude apostates from the Catholic communion. They also suppressed the stipends which were paid to the bishops and clergy as a compensation for the Church property of which the government had taken possession; but they held out a lure to the weak, promising payment to all who submitted. To drive the clergy to starvation they forbade any collections to be made for their support or the maintenance of divine worship. Lay elective commissions were created to manage Church property, and finally all religious orders of men and women, and even the Sisters of Charity, were suppressed.

Pius IX., at the very outset of these persecutions, addressed a note to the Prussian Government recalling the fidelity of the German Catholics to all their duties as citizens, and asking how it was possible that they could have become conspirators against its well-being. But his appeal was disregarded, and new severities were inflicted. The Prussian bishops could not yield. In May, 1873, they declared that the Church cannot recognize the pagan principle that the laws of the state are the source of all right, and the Church has only such rights as the state concedes to her. She cannot deny the divinity of her origin without making Christianity itself depend on the arbitrary will of men. Fines and imprisonment were now meted out to the doomed bishops and clergy, and a state tribunal assumed to depose them. The archbishop of Posen, the bishop of Paderborn, the prince bishop of Breslau and others still, were imprisoned. The bishops of England and the United States encouraged these confessors of the faith, and Pope Pius wrote personally to the Emperor William on the 7th of August, 1873; but the emperor replied with unworthy subterfuges, and showed his hearty approval of the whole system so disgraceful to a country where freedom of thought is claimed as a special right.

Finally, on the 5th of February, 1875, Pius IX., in an encyclical addressed to the Prussian bishops, encouraged them to constancy and patience, urging them to avoid anything that could be construed into a violation of any law not touching their religious rights, so as to give no pretext to their enemies. As the government was straining every nerve to intrude fallen priests of the old Catholic heresy into parishes by pretended elections, the Pope declared such intruders excommunicated *ipso facto*, and warned the faithful not to attend any mass or office celebrated by them, or accept their ministry for themselves or their children.

To the troubles arising from the persecutions at home and abroad, a private affliction befell Pope Pius IX. in 1872. His brother Count Cajetan Mastai died on the 20th of September, but his days of grief and mourning were not respected by Victor Emmanuel, who turned them into days of public noise and rejoicing.

The persecution of the Church in Switzerland resembled that in Prussia. The Protestant and infidel parties combined carried things even to further lengths. Having a majority in the legislature, and having after the Sonderbund deprived the Catholic cantons of the right of controlling their own religious affairs, the enemies of the Church abrogated the concordat concluded with the Pope in 1828, passed laws for the election of parish priests, and suppressed most of the parishes. In the Bernese Jura sixty-nine thousand non-Catholics imposed on the Catholic population of eighteen thousand a law for "the reorganization of the Catholic worship." The Catholics could not recognize such interference in their faith and discipline. The government then drove into exile Mgr. Mermillod, bishop of Hebron and coadjutor of Geneva, and deposed Bishop Lachat of Basle on the ground that he accepted the Vatican Council. Every one of the sixty-nine parish priests in the Bernese Jura was deposed, driven from his parish, and finally from the country. Disgraced priests from various parts flocked in, and were elected by non-Catholic votes and installed by government in the Catholic churches. The churches in Geneva, Berne, and other parts where the rights of Catholics were protected by treaty, were similarly wrested from the Catholics, who, prevented by their conscience from voting, saw a few Free Masons, or free-thinkers claiming to be Catholics seize their churches and install notorious apostates. Then the teachers who refused to attend the mock services of these wretches were driven from the schools. Catholics could hear mass only by stealth, or in barns and outhouses. Switzerland in all this was supported by Bismarck, who prevented the expelled priests from crossing the frontiers into his empire.

The Pope saw his nuncio dismissed, and all diplomatic relations broken off, so that his appeals to the sense of honor and justice of the ancient republic were of no effect. In his encyclical of November 21st he deplored the evils which had overtaken the Church in so many parts, and pointed to their true source, the secret societies. These, animated by a satanic hatred of Christian truth, had, by securing the administration in many countries, begun a terrible and unrelenting war on the Catholic Church, which they justly regarded as the only obstacle to their fell designs. By their use of the press they blinded masses of the people to believe them the real advocates of the best interests of man; but sooner or later the mask would fall, and this fearful anti-Christian conspiracy stand before the world in its true hideousness. In this encyclical he again condemned the sacrilegious usurpers of the patrimony of St. Peter; he praised the constancy of the exiled Swiss bishops and their faithful clergy, while he excommunicated formally the intruded priests. As to the laws of Prussia against the Church, he declared them to be such as could possess no binding force on the conscience of Catholics. As the persecution continued with unrelenting severity, Pius IX., on the 23d of March, 1875, addressed another encyclical to the Swiss bishops and clergy, stigmatizing the movements of the so-called Old Catholics of which they were the victims.

The Sacred College of Cardinals had by death been greatly reduced in numbers. From time to time the Pope had raised to this exalted position members of the episcopate or clergy whose services foreshadowed a fitness for that great Council of the Church. In 1863 he appointed Cardinal Panebianco of the Order of St. Francis, Cardinal Trevisanato, patriarch of Venice, Cardinals de Luca and Bizzari, Archbishop Sastra of Seville, Archbishop Bonnechose of Rouen, Dom Pitra of the Order of St. Benedict. In his creation of June

22, 1866, he conferred the cardinal's hat for the first time on a native of Ireland, and a dignitary in the Island of Saints. The long constancy and sufferings of Ireland were rewarded by seeing His Grace Paul Cullen, Archbishop of Dublin, take his place in the Sacred College, the only other cardinal appointed at the time being Gustavus von Hohenlohe, a prince of one of the highest houses in Germany. Six cardinals were created in 1868, among them Lucian Bonaparte, and John Ignatius Moreno, a native of Guatemala. On the 22d of December, 1873, Pius IX. raised to the same dignity a number of archbishops in various countries, and an humble Jesuit, Father Tarquini, who did not live long to enjoy the unsought honor.

The Church was soon to meet persecution in a new field. In Brazil discipline had been so relaxed that many confraternities connected with the churches had admitted persons, who, as members of the Masonic lodges and other secret societies, could not approach the sacraments, being in fact no longer Catholics. The bishops wished to revive piety and make these confraternities, what they were in their origin, associations of zealous, practical Catholics, frequenters of the sacraments. This became all the more necessary as Masonry made open war on religion. Bishop Oliveira, of Olinda, called upon the confraternities to expel all members of the secret societies forbidden by the Church. They refused, and the bishop interdicted their chapels. On this they appealed to the civil courts, composed mainly of Free Masons; these ordered the bishop to remove the interdict, and on his denying the competence of the state tribunals to decide a purely ecclesiastical question, he was sentenced to imprisonment and hard labor. It is almost inconceivable that in a pretendedly Catholic country such a monstrous mockery of

justice could be perpetrated. But the
bishop of Olinda was seized in January,
1874, and carried on a man-of-war to Rio
Janeiro, where he was confined in an unhealthy prison under the very eyes of the
emperor, who sustained the whole iniquity. The bishop of Para soon met the
same fate; and the administrators of the
two dioceses, for refusing to raise the interdict, were also sent to prison.

Failing to crush the independence of
the episcopate by brute force, they attempted to surprise the good faith of the
Pope, and the Brazilian Government sent
a delegate to Rome to misrepresent the
conduct of the bishops as rash, illegal, and
detrimental to the faith. But there was
Catholic feeling left in Brazil, and the
elections that followed drove from office
the ministry; the bishops were set at liberty, and Pius IX., on delusive promises,
allowed the interdicts to be removed. It
is needless to say, however, that faith has

not been kept, and that the original difficulty still remains.

Venezuela attempted the Prussian and Swiss system; Buenos Ayres in a riot destroyed a college of the Jesuit Fathers; Peru claimed all the *jus patronatus* of the Spanish kings, and Pius IX., to avoid greater evils, granted this under certain necessary restrictions by his brief in March, 1874.

Ecuador alone in those lands gave real consolation to the heart of the Pope. There the noble Garcia Moreno sought to elevate his people by giving the Church freedom to do her work. He sent ten thousand dollars to the prisoner of the Vatican in the name of the Republic of Ecuador; he consecrated that State to the Sacred Heart of Jesus; he gave shelter to religious expelled from Switzerland. Ecuador was instinct with new life. With a clergy full of zeal, not appointed by the president from political motives, as in Peru, but chosen by the bishops for merit and learning, a spirit of faith and intelligence would have soon been diffused. The revolution doomed him. Moreno was assassinated in August, 1875.

Russia was a constant source of grief to Pius IX. He had never been able to obtain any relaxation of the persecution of the United Greeks, and from time to time the Latin Church in that empire suffered as well. The Archbishop of Warsaw, Mgr. Felinski, and other bishops had been exiled to Siberia in 1863; priests died and none replaced them; churches were seized.

Nicholas had, by his course of cruelties, driven whole communities of United Greeks into the schismatic Russian Church. The little diocese of Chelm remained, and on this the fury of Alexander II. was turned. The horrors told in Catholic journals found none to believe them, but they have been made patent to the world in an official publication of the English Government. The rosary, preaching in

Polish, organs, bells, and monstrances were first abolished by law. Bishop Kalinski of Chelm, opposing these changes, was sent to Siberia, and died there in the arms of the bishop of Wilna, a fellow exile. The government sent one Popiel as administrator, who forced schismatic priests into the churches. The faithful were driven into the edifices with the knout, and every refusal punished by heavy fines; many died of their injuries and of starvation; numbers were sent to Siberia. As this failed, a new course was adopted. A priest named Kuzienski was nominated for the see of Chelm, and as nothing was known against him the Pope appointed him. He at once sided with the government till, overcome by remorse, he retired to Galicia, leaving Popiel again in full control. By the order of that man the United Greek service was made to conform in all respects to the schismatic. The peasants endeavored to keep out the schismatic priests from their churches. Numbers were accordingly shot down by the Cossacks at Pratulin, and Drylow. In the autumn of 1874 the persecution revived with all its violence.

Pius IX. conjured the United Greek archbishop of Lemberg in Austrian Poland to do all in his power to relieve those poor people who could not escape from the country even. By his bull *Omnem Solicitudinem* (May 13, 1874), he declared that the Holy See had always esteemed the Eastern liturgies, and especially that of the United Greeks, as adjusted by the Council of Zamosc, in 1720. This was communicated to the poor people, but the Russians perverted it in every way, and the violence continued till numbers yielded. Then it was proclaimed that the diocese of Chelm had returned to the orthodox Greek faith. Alexander refused all petitions and appeals, created a new diocese of Lublin, and appointed Popiel bishop. The United Greek Church in Russia was thus absolutely crushed out of existence, in open violation of treaties guaranteeing its adherents the free exercise of their faith.

The war has now begun on the Latin churches; many have been suppressed, the Latin clergy are forbidden to baptize children of parents belonging to the Latin and United Greek rites, and all tends to show that fearful persecutions will follow.

Amid all these distresses in various parts of his vast flock the aged Pope had little to console him. His twenty-eighth anniversary was hailed with joy on the 20th of June, 1874, but he was grieved to see those who manifested their devotion to him arrested in the streets of Rome and dragged to prison as criminals. So had the law of guarantees been kept which pretended to secure the same honors to the Pope as to the king!

His allocution in the Consistory of December 21st deplored the schism among the Armenians and the Chaldeans in the Turkish empire, which, fomented by Germany, was causing great injury to souls. On the eve of Christmas he proclaimed the Jubilee for 1875. This led to a general revival of faith and piety. Pilgrimages to the shrines famous for graces received—Lourdes, Paray le Monial, Rome, Loretto, Einsiedeln—became numerous and fervent. The Eternal City saw bodies of the faithful arrive constantly to pray at the tombs of the Apostles, and the spots hallowed by the lives and deaths of so many saints; and few departed without visiting the Vatican to receive the blessing of the Holy Father.

Against him the so-called Italian Government sought new arrows. It prohibited the papers from printing his words, addresses, allocutions, or the like. It passed laws to force seminarians to serve in the army. To save them Pius IX. appealed to Victor Emmanuel, but in vain.

In a promotion of cardinals in May, 1875, Pius IX. bestowed the cardinal's hat on Archbishop Ledochowski, of Posen, then in prison in Germany; on the illustrious Manning, Archbishop of Westminster, on the Archbishops of Mechlin, Chalcedon, Rennes, and Sardia, and on the Patriarch of Constantinople. To America, too, he paid a high honor in giving the Church in the Western World for the first time an American cardinal, American not only in birth, but in the dignity he already possessed. To the joy of the whole Catholic population of the United States he raised to the dignity of cardinal-priest John McCloskey, Archbishop of New York, whose gentleness of character, zeal, and labors in his priesthood, as Coadjutor of New York, Bishop of Albany, and Archbishop of New York, had endeared him to all.

The feeling of gratitude for this high

JOHN, CARDINAL McCLOSKEY.
Born March 10, 1810.
Created Cardinal, March 15, 1875.

honor was not confined to Catholics. In fact the first known proposal for the creation of an American cardinal was made during the presidency of Abraham Lincoln, by the American minister to Rome. Pius IX. then remarked, that as he was the first pope who had ever been in America, it was right that he should appoint the first American cardinal. This project was at last effected, and the government of the United States thanked his Holiness for thus enabling the Catholics of the Union to be represented in the great Council of the Church.

On the 6th of November, 1876, Pius IX. sustained a great loss. God in his providence took from him one who had for years been his trusted minister, the wise and able Cardinal Antonelli, a man of unblemished life, a devoted servant of the See of Peter, a statesman of that rare stamp that is rarely met in history. In all the difficulties that chequered the pontificate of Pope Pius IX., Cardinal Antonelli had shown genius of the highest order. The diplomatic body, so frequently in relation with him, attested the grandeur of his mind, the nobility and truly Christian character of his policy in an age that seeks to divorce statesmanship from religion.

This great man was born at Sonnino, April 2, 1806, of a family which had long possessed means and position among their fellow-citizens. Devoting himself to the service of the Church he studied with a view to a position in the prelacy, and held several judicial and executive offices. Not long after his accession Pope Pius IX. made him Under Secretary of State. In 1847 he became Minister of Finance and President of the Ministry, and from that time to his death served the Pope with all his remarkable talents and ability. He was, as we have seen, made a cardinal-deacon, but never was ordained a priest.

Possessing great wealth from his family, and fine tastes, his hours of relaxation were spent among the artistic collections which he had gathered around him.

The more recent acts of the great Pope, his allocution of December 25, 1875, his action in regard to the attempted violation of the Spanish Concordat, his brief to the Brazilian bishops on the Masonic body on the 27th of May, 1876, and his brief to the bishop of St. Paul, in August, merit the attention of all.

In China, though treaties had been made with the Catholic powers, which guaranteed the Church from persecution, Pius IX. beheld the vanity of trusting in princes. The Emperor of China was too weak or too hostile to carry out the treaties in good faith. From time to time sad tidings reach us from that strange realm. Scarcely had reparation been made for the massacre of Catholics at Tientsin, where devoted priests and sisters with their faithful converts dyed the soil with their blood, when a new persecution broke out. A Catholic catechist was put to death in April, 1876, at Kiengpinkien, and a native Chinese priest, Wang, was soon after put to death at Ningkofou.

While the heralds of the truth of God were thus witnessing with their blood in China, devoted French priests, endeavoring to remove the darkness from the heart of Africa and let the beams of the Sun of Justice illumine that pagan-bound land, fell victims to their zeal, receiving the crown of martyrdom at the hands of the ruthless Touaregs.

In April, 1876, the Pope promoted to the Sacred College the bishop of Calvi, Mgr. Bartholomew d'Avanzi, and Father Franzelin, of the Society of Jesus.

In the consistory of March 12, 1877, Pius IX. raised to the Sacred College the Patriarch of the West Indies, the Archbishops of Capua, Saragossa, Neo Cæsarea, Compostella, and Lyons, the Bishops of Verona, Viterbo, as cardinal priests, and three prelates, Mgrs. Nina, Sbarreti, and Falloux, as cardinal deacons.

In his allocution he reviewed all that the Church had suffered since the moment when, seven years before, the invaders of his civil principality, breaking faith in solemn compacts, and taking advantage of the misfortunes of an illustrious Catholic nation, by violence and force of arms occupied the provinces still remaining in his power, and took possession of the holy city.

He recounted their false and worthless promises, the suppression of religious orders whose work was absolutely necessary for the transaction of the affairs of ecclesiastical congregations, and for the performance of so many of the duties of our ministry. This fatal suppression struck even the colleges established in

Rome for holy missions, for the training of worthy laborers, willing fearlessly to bear the light of the Gospel even into the most remote and barbarous regions. Thus they deprived many nations of the saving succors of piety and charity, to the great detriment of human welfare and civilization, both of which spring from the holiness, the teachings, and the virtues of our religion.

He spoke of the laws in the pretendedly free country which prevented men or women from living together beneath the same roof, if actuated by religious motives; of the law by which young seminarians were torn from the schools of divinity, and forced into the army, of the seizure of the Church property, and the profanation of sacred buildings, and the gradual suppression of all those pious works and institutions which were the pride of Catholic Rome.

He then enlarged upon the daring

"Law on Clerical Abuses" which had already passed one house. "Once this law is passed and promulgated," says the Pope, "a lay tribunal will be permitted to define whether, in the administration of the sacraments, and in the preaching of the Word of God, the priest has disturbed and how he has disturbed the public conscience and the peace of families; and the condition of the bishop and priest will be such that their voices can be restricted and silenced, equally with that of the Vicar of Jesus Christ, who, although declared in his person, through political reasons, exempt from all penalties, is none the less supposed to be punished in the person of those who may have been accomplices in his fault. This is, in fact, what a minister of the kingdom in the Chamber of Duputies did not hesitate to declare openly, when, speaking of us, he freely avowed that it was neither new nor obsolete in the laws, nor contrary to the rules, the science, or the practice of criminal law, to punish the accomplices in a crime when the chief author could not be reached. Whence it becomes clear that in the intention of those who govern, it is against our person, also, that the force of this law is directed; so that when our words or acts shall come in contact with this law, the bishops or priests who may have repeated our words, or executed our orders, must suffer the penalty of the pretended crime, of which we, as chief author, will be condemned to bear the inculpation of the offense."

He then refuted those who pretended that he was not a prisoner, because he was allowed to receive deputations of bishops and priests; he detailed all that was done and permitted to degrade religion, to prevent any public religious manifestations by pilgrimages or processions. He shows that he must regard as a piece of bitter irony and a mere mockery the assertion that he ought to take measures to conciliate the new masters, by yielding up to them not only his sworn rights as sovereign, but in reality his divine ministry as head of the Church, to be exercised in such matters as suited for the time being the creatures who might for the moment have the control in that one country of earth.

He concluded with these forcible words: "Now every one can certainly see, in all their manifestness, and under all their phases, the force, the vigor, and the good faith of those pretended guarantees, by means of which, to deceive the faithful, our enemies have boasted of meaning to secure the freedom and dignity of the Roman Pontiff, and which are at the mere mercy of the hostile whims and caprices of the governments on which they depend, according to their plans, their purposes, and the pleasure of their whims, to apply, preserve, interpret, and execute. Never, most assuredly never, can the Roman Pontiff ever be fully master of his freedom and his power, so long as he remains subject to the rulers in his capital. There is no other destiny possible for him in Rome but that of a sovereign or a prisoner; and there can never be any peace, security, or tranquillity for the entire Catholic Church so long as the exercise of the supreme ecclesiastical ministry is at the mercy of the passions of party, the caprice of governments, the vicissitudes of political elections, and of the projects and actions of designing men who will not hesitate to sacrifice justice to their own interests."

But the great Pope was full of hope, and thanking the faithful who, in their charity, had come forward so generously to meet the wants of the Church, he urged all to pray for the speedy deliverance of the Spouse of Christ.

The usurping government at once issued a circular, in which, though they scarcely ventured yet to prevent the publication of the allocution or threaten violence to the Holy Father, they forbade any paper to add to the allocution any comments expressing their adhesion to the words of the Pope.

Cardinal Simeoni at once addressed a circular to all the apostolic nuncios representing the Holy See, in which, after a magnificent defense of the Holy See, he called special attention to this act of the so-called Italian Government, and to the position of the Pope. This circular, laid before the various courts, drew at once clear and decisive expressions of opinion. Even the liberal press of England at last admitted that the Pope was absolutely right, and Victor Emmanuel and his government utterly in the wrong.

We have thus sketched the life of Pius IX. from his earliest years, and especially of his career as Pope and king. Events have shown that the zeal for a united

Italy was rooted mainly in a hatred of the Catholic Church. The party whom we have called the Revolution, whether the commune in Paris or Bismarck in Berlin, or Victor Emmanuel in Rome, whether from the dregs of society or the throne and the cabinet, may profess great love for humanity and hold forth glittering promises, but when we look for results we find nothing effected except oppression of the Catholic Church. People will soon ask themselves, What has liberalism done for Spain, for Italy, for Germany? Are the people advanced in well-being, education, morality? The absolute sterility of all result will but set in a higher luster the just claims of the Catholic Church as the greatest institution the world has ever beheld for the well-being of nations.

In the great contest in which liberalism, wielding all the brute force that government machinery can grasp, has warred upon the Church, Pius IX. stands in moral grandeur as the unconquered, vigilant, zealous leader of the hosts of Israel. Never compromising the cause of truth and justice, undismayed by peril, unshaken in trial, he is and has long been and we trust long will be to the enemies of the faith a grim citadel of firmness, while to the faithful he is all that can win their affectionate devotion and loyalty.

On Sunday, June 3, 1877, the Catholic world united with its glorious Pontiff in commemorating his consecration as bishop in the church of "St. Peter in Chains," fifty years before. Preparations had been made in all countries for the day; bishops and priests, religious and laymen, bent their way to Rome, and every diocese sent its offering to lay at the feet of the imprisoned Pope. During the month of May, deputation after deputation reached Rome to offer addresses and gifts. More than a million of dollars attested the love, devotion, and generosity of his world-wide flock; and it is gratifying to state, that if France, so active in all good works, led the list, the hierarchy of the United States, scarcely older than the Pope, stood second on the list, surpassing all other countries.

When the eventful day dawned upon Rome, immense crowds gathered in the basilica of St. Peter in Chains—that ancient church where only a year before the relics of the Seven Machabee Brothers were discovered—to celebrate the anniversary. A large painting over the main entrance represented the solemn consecration of fifty years before, and an elegant Latin inscription expressed the thanks of the Catholic world to God for preserving Pius IX. to rule in the Church of God, as well as the fervent prayer of the city and the world that, as Prince and Pontiff, he might yet crown the triumph of the Catholic cause. Within all was light and decoration. Over the main arch, on a cloth of gold, was the inscription, "Thou shalt sanctify the fiftieth year, for it is the jubilee of the Lord." On the gospel side was a text as apposite: "Jerusalem, lift up thy eyes round about and see: All these are gathered together, thy sons have come to thee." On the epistle side, "Thy sons shall come to thee from afar, bringing gold and frankincense, and announcing the praise of the Lord." Portraits of twenty-two great bishops, revered as saints, hung around. The solemn high mass was celebrated by Cardinal Simeoni, in the presence of several members of the Sacred College, many bishops and prelates, the Duke and Duchess of Parma, the ambassadors of France and Austria, and many distinguished individuals. The music of Palestrini, rendered as only Rome can render it, moved all hearts.

The line of carriages that soon after were seen proceeding to the Vatican seemed endless; the streets were thronged, and though the usurpers hung out on their government buildings the Italian flag, they found scarce an imitator in the city.

The Sala Ducale in the Vatican was crowded; more than three thousand Italians had come to attest their fidelity to Pius IX. and the Papacy; and when at one o'clock the Pope, who had celebrated his Jubilee mass in his private chapel, appeared, he was greeted with enthusiastic cries: "Viva Pio Nono! Viva el Pontifice, il Re! Ad multos annos! Viva, viva, il Beatissimo Padre!"

The Holy Father was at first too deeply moved to find utterance for words. Then he said: "My beloved children, when I see so many of you, and I know you are not all here, I feel great consolation and great joy, because you are the evidences of what Catholic Italy really is. And like Jacob I bless my children. I bless them, that their numbers may increase

POPE PIUS IX.,
IN THE ACT OF GIVING HIS PONTIFICIAL BENEDICTION TO THE WORLD AT THE
CELEBRATION OF HIS GOLDEN JUBILEE.

still more, so that being united in heart and faith, this faith and this union may increase with numbers for your welfare, for general edification, and for the triumph of the Church. I bless you, your families, your societies, your dioceses, so that this benediction may be a tower of strength to you in the struggles of this life, while waiting for the endless joys of eternity."

All knelt during his impressive words, but rose with renewed enthusiasm as he retired.

Addresses of congratulation from all countries were presented, that from the United States by Archbishop Wood of Philadelphia; while the offerings of the faithful formed an international exhibition.

The whole city was full of signs of devotion, and the trembling usurper called out his troops to the number of thousands for a review, and sent his lowest rabble to yell insults to the Pope through the streets; but nothing could check the ardor of the real Romans. When night fell the palaces of the Roman princes and others devoted to Pope Pius IX. were illuminated in token of the general joy.

This Jubilee was soon followed by the thirty-first anniversary of his elevation to the See of Peter, and he thus enters on a new year of that Pontificate which has wrought such wonders for the Church.

CHAPTER XV.

PERSONAL APPEARANCE OF PIUS IX.—HIS MODE OF LIFE.—SUPERNATURAL GIFTS ASCRIBED TO HIM.—CONCLUSION.

PIUS IX. is in stature rather above middle size, his head is large and his forehead broad and high, his hair is white, his complexion very clear, and still rosy in the cheeks, his lips red and rather large; his quick black eyes, though very soft, light up his whole countenance. His head habitually inclines slightly to the right.

His voice is gentle, yet sonorous; in conversation its harmony enchants all, and in the great ceremonies of the Church it rises with singular power and beauty in the vast temples of religion, full of dignity and grandeur.

His life is most simple. While he has spent millions in charitable institutions, especially on orphanages, on churches and their adornment, on the collections of the Vatican, all that he personally requires is an official room and a sleeping-chamber. The last is uncarpeted; plain yellow curtains hang at the windows. His bedstead is a small iron one without curtains, and this constitutes almost the entire furniture of the room, with the prie dieu on which stands his crucifix. No fire is ever lighted there, cold as the weather may be. His sitting-room is small, with a table covered by a plain cloth, two chairs, an arm-chair, and a book-case.

Ever since his elevation to the Pontificate his course of life has been uniform. Unless after unusual fatigue, or by direction of his physician, he rises at half-past five, and dresses without assistance from his attendant.

After his morning prayer in his room, he proceeds to his little chapel, where he remains for half an hour before the Blessed Sacrament. He then says his mass and hears another while making his thanksgiving. When he is not well enough to celebrate, he hears a mass said by one of his chaplains and receives Holy Communion.

He then gives directions in any urgent matter that will not admit of delay, recites his office, and about nine o'clock takes a cup of black coffee, which is his whole breakfast, and his whole morning refreshment unless on days of unusual fatigue, when he allows himself a cup of light soup. During his breakfast, members of his family who may happen to be in Rome are received in audience. The morning letters are then received, for the mail is brought to his Holiness three times a day, and he not only opens the bag himself, but opens every letter addressed from all parts of the world, and notes in his own hand instructions for his secretary to draw up the answer. In this way no letter of importance ever remains in the Pope's desk at night.

The Cardinal Secretary of State is next received in audience, and on his retirement those persons who have obtained special introductions are admitted, often taking up the whole time till half-past ten o'clock, when the doors of the grand apartments are opened to receive the cardinal prefects of the various congregations, who wait upon the Pope to discuss the general affairs of the Church, and also ministers and other dignitaries for whom audiences have been assigned. Next follow the private audiences of those who have obtained that honor. Except on solemn occasions when the throne-room is used, Pius IX. receives them in his simple study.

When the audiences are over, the Pope retires for a time to the chapel to pray before Him whose representative he is on earth. After this he spends a short time in conversation with his chamberlains, and at half-past two dinner is served.

According to Pontifical etiquette the Pope usually dines alone, although exception is at times made in favor of princes or princesses. He is served by his first valet de chambre. The meal consists of soup, a piece of boiled beef, a broil or roast, one dish of vegetables and one of fruit. On days of fasting and abstinence, fish and white meats replace the flesh meats; but no better fare is provided for holidays. He takes a little ordinary white wine, greatly diluted with water, and his supply is purchased day by day, for Pius IX. has no wine cellar. When very weary he takes after his dinner a glass of wine, furnished especially by the Sisters of St. Joseph at Bourdeaux, made from a vineyard named after the Pope and cultivated with their own hands.

All other delicacies offered him, and they are not few, are sent to the hospital. He never touches pastry or preserves.

After dinner he takes a siesta of a quarter of an hour in an arm-chair.

His next occupation is to say his beads, and recite vespers and complin. After this Pius IX., in other times, drove out to one of the great promenades of Rome; and this moment of the day was anxiously looked for by visitors to the Eternal City, who wished to see the Pope. The favored ranged themselves on each side of the gallery through which he passed to his carriage in his white cassock, red cape, and hat. A dragoon riding in advance announced his coming, and a line was formed on either side of the streets to receive his blessing. When he reached the appointed destination for the day, it was the custom of Pius IX. to alight and mingle with the crowd, exchanging kind words with any whom he recognized, and these were always many, for he possesses a wonderful memory, and recollects almost every one presented to him.

Now of course that he is a prisoner this is impossible, and the very fact is one of the strong proofs that he is actually a prisoner. In spite of the guarantees proposed by Mazzini and carried out by Victor Emmanuel, the Pope is so completely under the surveillance of the police that, on the occasion of his twenty-eighth anniversary in 1874, when he appeared at a window in the Vatican, and the rapturous *vivas* arose among the people, all who

INTERIOR OF THE PANTHEON, NOW CHURCH OF SANCTA MARIA AD MARTYRES.

thus showed their attachment were arrested and punished. For the few then assembled, there would be tens of thousands who would crowd to hail the Pope, were he to drive out as of old through the streets of Rome, and the King of Sardinia would either shoot down the people or leave the city to its true ruler.

Now the Pope takes his promenade in the galleries or in the gardens of the Vatican, where one alley lined with orange trees is his favorite resort. He is fond of sitting beneath a weeping willow at its extremity near the Zitella fountain, and throwing crumbs to some beautiful white pigeons kept there.

Notwithstanding his advanced age his step is firm and quick, and his cane seems not required as a support. He sometimes laughs at his own activity, as he waits for the younger companions of his promenades.

In other days he frequently walked out, and was most happy to find himself among the poor, whom he could relieve and console, or children whom he could question and encourage; for his early interest in the young, shown at Tata Giovanni, has never decreased, and if in the future he should ever be placed on our altars, he will be the patron of the children of the poor.

Rome is full of anecdotes of his kindness to those in humble circumstances, of his remembrance of all who rendered him service, of the affectionate intercourse between him and the young.

The Pope returns to his rooms at the Angelus, and after reciting matins and lauds of the next day with one of his chaplains, used formerly to give audiences on matters connected with his government. At nine o'clock he takes his frugal supper, consisting of a plate of soup, two potatoes, and a single fruit. At ten o'clock precisely he retires to his room, after a visit to the Blessed Sacrament.

There is pomp in the great functions where the Pope appears as Pontiff or king; but in his private life, what can be conceived more simple, more poor, more frugal, more pious than this daily life of Pope Pius IX.? The greatness is the greatness of his position; the firmness is the firmness of duty; in person he is simple, temperate, unostentatious; and this simple, holy life, upborne by the spirit of prayer and confidence in almighty God, makes him a power which all the efforts of the world to crush only exalt.

Many of those separated from our faith profess to think the change at Rome for the best; but not one in his heart will say that the new ruler as a man in all that constitutes a pure, good man can be compared to Pius IX.; not one will show by facts that Rome and the Papal States are better governed, or that the general happiness of the people has been increased. If the change gives these States an inferior ruler, a less successful government, why should it stand?

In the eyes of a Catholic such a comparison is almost an insult to one who is not only beloved as a wronged and persecuted high-priest of God, but revered as one whose life is so holy in the sight of heaven that the Almighty makes him the channel of supernatural favors. From time to time cures and other remarkable graces are reported as having been obtained by the prayers, the blessing, or the touch of something belonging to Pius IX. If any juridical examination has been made in these cases it is not communicated to the public, and we cannot, therefore, attest the facts. But they are believed by thousands who have witnessed and examined them, and in themselves attest the deep-seated feeling in Catholic hearts that God would grant extraordinary favors solicited through his servant.

It cannot be said that Catholics always

look upon the Pope as a saint; their respect for his high dignity has nothing in common with that instinct of the Catholic heart which in rare cases fixes upon a person as a saint raised above the ordinary level of the good and pious, moving as it were on another plane, Elias-like still living, but associated with the glorified.

Among the cases to which we refer were those of Mr. Bodenham, of London, restored on his death-bed, at the moment, in 1865, when the Pope united his prayers with those of the dying man; of a paralyzed novice at Digne cured in August, 1866, and a young man at Paris, similarly paralyzed, cured in the same year by applying a stocking worn by the Pope. In 1875 a lady of the Sacred Heart at Rome, whose right arm was paralyzed, obtained an audience of the Pope, and when he raised the afflicted limb and bade her make the sign of the cross, she did so and found herself completely cured.

One day when Pius IX. entered the Hospital of San Spirito, a mason who had fallen from a building was brought in to all appearance dead. He was utterly unconscious, and a cloth was laid over his face, so persuaded were all that the soul had left the body. The Pope went up and removed it. He blessed the senseless form and said, "Do you hear me, my son?" Not the slightest tremor betrayed the presence of life; he lay still and silent. "Make the sign of the cross," said the Pope. To the wonder of all, the man not only made the sign but pronounced the words. "Here, my son," said Pius IX., "here is something to help you live till you are completely well," giving him a considerable alms. The poor man thanked the Holy Father over and over, and Pius IX. blessing him again went his way. The next morning the mason was taken home, and another day saw him completely restored.

When any of these cases are referred to the Pope always turns the conversation off with one of his pleasantries. So when the young Parisian in his gratitude hastened to Rome, and having obtained an audience, burst forth in expressions of thanks, Pius IX. laughingly remarked, "That is very strange; all my trouble is in my legs, and though I wear my stockings all day they do not cure me."

We have thus traced the life of the present Pope from his birth to his entrance upon the thirty-second year of his pontificate. It may seem to some that our words have been simply those of eulogy, that we have painted all in brightest colors, and have in their brightness made the shades disappear. But we have indulged in no exaggerations. The tongue of slander has never assailed the personal character of Pius IX. Nothing unbecoming a young Christian gentleman has ever been raked up from real or imaginary sources to throw a shade over his early manhood. The clumsy invention that he was admitted into a condemned secret society is the only charge, and in this country we need little proof to show it an invention. The devoted young priest and the archbishop stand equally untarnished. As Pope King, no ruler sought more actively and honestly the greatest good of the people of his States, ruled with greater justice, mercy, economy: as head of the Church his course has met the enthusiastic adherence of the whole body of the faithful.

That in his own self-examination he finds steps that may have ill-judged, something for self-reproach, cannot but be true, for the Pope like every other child of the Church kneels at the foot of his confessor to avow his faults: but history shows no more unblemished character through a long and active life.

The life of Pope Pius IX. is not closed,

and the prayers of millions ascend to heaven, that the life so wonderfully prolonged may still be extended to permit him to behold the triumph of right and truth. His pontificate has been one marked by commemorations; he has celebrated not only the twenty-fifth, but the thirty-first anniversary of his election; the fiftieth of his priesthood, the fiftieth of his episcopate. Born when religion seemed prostrate in France; crushed in England; fettered and weakened in Germany; when in the United States a bishop, with the whole country for his diocese, was just endeavoring to see what could be done to save the few Catholics in the land, Pius IX. has lived to see the Church, like an army ranged in array, battling, but full of life, earnestness, and zeal, meeting the enemy at every point, growing stronger by being ever under arms, encouraged by his words and zeal and sufferings and great deeds, inspired by tokens of Heaven's approval, the apparitions of Our Lady at La Salette, Lourdes, and Marpingen, the wonders wrought there reviving pilgrimages throughout the world, the living image of the Crucified in Louise Lateau, the extended devotion to the Sacred Heart encouraged by the beatification of the Blessed Margaret Mary Alacoque, pilgrimages to Paray-le-Monial, and his own consecration of the whole Church and every diocese to our loving Redeemer under that same consoling title. He has seen it under his eyes united more closely than ever, its doctrines made definite and distinct by his decrees and those of a General Council. The priest who sought the children of the people, as Pope has made the Catholic body feel that its strength lay not in the favor of kings and princes, but in the hearts and the energy and devotedness of the Catholic people throughout the world.

FATHER BURKE ON PIUS IX.

AMONGST all the people that in their many languages come to lay their tribute of one faith and one love at the aged Pontiff's feet, where is the nation and where is the race that has so good a right to sympathize with him as Ireland and her people? On two great grounds I establish that claim, and that peculiar privilege of sympathy. The first ground is, that amongst the nations that send their sons to Rome, to the feet of the Pontifical throne, there is not one that has kept the faith with greater purity and in a firmer grasp than Ireland. We have kept the faith. When the Apostle of the Gentiles was about to approach his death, he gave thanks to God for many high and great favors bestowed upon him, and of those that he mentioned, the greatest was expressed in these words: "I thank thee, O my God, that I have kept the faith." Ireland has kept the faith as pure, as strong, grand, and as fruitful in holiness and in purity to-day as when our fathers received it from the hands of Patrick and from his holy lips, and sprung from being a nation of pagans to be a nation of saints. Our second privilege and claim to that magnificent office of sympathizing with the Holy Father lies in this: that we, also, have suffered. No man can sympathize with a sufferer for justice so well as the man who has himself suffered for justice' sake. It was written, and well written:

"Haud ignora mali miseris succurrere disco."

When the Son of God himself called upon his Virgin Mother to sustain him in his last hour by the strength of her sympathy, he called upon her in the hour of her deepest sorrow, and it was not so much as Queen of Virgins, or Queen of Angels, but it was as Queen of Sorrows we behold her standing by her dying God on the cross. And Ireland is the Queen of Sorrows among the nations. She is the Niobe of nations, but her tears were of blood; the Niobe of nations, but she never wept away the grand love that was in her heart, and her heart's blood beats as strong and as vigorous to-day as on the day when she first girded up her virgin loins, and stood her three hundred years of martyrdom for God and for his anointed.

Now the question is, In what do we sympathize with our Holy Father? We sympathize with him in the many trials he has endured. I have more or less a special right to speak of this, for I remember, when I first went to Rome, in 1847, Pius IX. coming out of the Church of the Jesuits to bless the people; but there was not a gray hair on his head, and the light of strength and manly beauty beamed from his kindly eyes. And I have lived for twelve years in the happiness of his presence and under his very hand, and I have seen him exalted by the people from whose hands he struck, in his greatness of soul, the chains of their slavery. I have heard him applauded to the skies by the people to whom he gave the very privilege which the modern idea of freedom claims for the people; and I have seen him again, as he returned from his exile at Gaeta, and a few short years—only three—had seemed to add half a century to the life of the man, for the heart within seemed broken, and he was stooped and bent, and even then the silver hair of sorrow was already whitening prematurely his young head. And I thought, on that day, if this continues, the man must die. And it has continued, and trial has been added to trial, and cross to cross; but the man raised himself upon the power of God, and he has borne more than ever a Pope, since Peter was imprisoned in Rome, has had to bear, and yet has outlived the longest life of any Pope that has ever reigned. We sympathize with him in that he is assailed in his independence—in that independence which is so necessary for him, but not for him so much as for us, that you, sons of the Church, may have free access to the Church's great Father, Governor, Chief, and Supreme Pontiff; and that no man shall be allowed to stand between the children and their great father.

The Pope was a king. He was a king by the grandest of titles, and a king who obtained his temporal sovereignty most legitimately, and who exercised that temporal sovereignty most beneficially, but who was deprived of it most shamefully. I do not go back to the principles of that fifth century, a thousand years ago. I appeal to those magnificent principles that we are accustomed to be bowing down to and bending our knees to in this nineteenth century of ours—"plebescite"—popular election, "Vox populi Dei, vox Dei," so often *Vox et præterea nihil.* Testing his temporal sovereignty even by the principles of the age in which we live, what do we find?

We find holy St. Gregory the Great lamenting for the Roman people in their desolation and their misery. Neglected and oppressed by the Court of Constantinople, misgoverned and misruled by the Exarchates, they have come to him as Lazarus came to the rich man's gate, to beg of him, for the love of God, to save their lives, that he would consent to be their king, and take up the temporal government of them. Yes, it began in the very hearts of the people, from the popular voice and from the right hand of the people, and if they had any right to give it, it was from them, under God, that the Pope got it.

The power thus gained legitimately was exercised beneficially. But that which he acquired so legitimately, that which he exercised, on the whole, so beneficially, he lost in our own day most shamefully. His spiritual sovereignty is not the only sovereignty of which the world cannot deprive Pius IX. There is another privilege which belongs to him. There is another tribute that will be paid to him and to his successors until the end of time, of which no violent hand can ever rob them, and that is the tribute, the privilege that we come to fulfill and to offer at his feet to-day, namely, the united hearts, the united intellects, the united homage and love of all the Catholic people of the whole world, and foremost among them the great and glorious people of Ireland.

www.ingramcontent.com/pod-product-compliance
Lightning Source LLC
Chambersburg PA
CBHW032005300426
44117CB00008B/901